KILL BILLS!

KILL BILLS!

THE 9 INSIDER TRICKS YOU NEED TO WIN THE WAR ON HOUSEHOLD BILLS

JOEL GIBSON

SIMON & SCHUSTER

London · New York · Sydney · Toronto · New Delhi

A CBS COMPANY

KILL BILLS!: The 9 insider tricks you need to win the war on household bills
First published in Australia in 2019 by
Simon & Schuster (Australia) Pty Limited
Suite 19A, Level 1, Building C, 450 Miller Street, Cammeray, NSW 2062

10 9 8 7 6 5 4 3 2 1

A CBS Company
Sydney New York London Toronto New Delhi
Visit our website at www.simonandschuster.com.au

Neither Simon & Schuster nor the author have any affiliation to, sponsorship with or authorisation from Quentin Tarantino, or from any of the writers, actors or producers of the Kill Bill *movies.*

NATIONAL LIBRARY OF AUSTRALIA

A catalogue record for this book is available from the National Library of Australia

Cover design: Luke Causby, Blue Cork
Internal illustrations by Rocco Fazzari
Photo on p. 59: Alicia Perera, *The West Australian*
Typeset by Midland Typesetters, Australia
Printed and bound in Australia by Griffin Press

FSC www.fsc.org MIX Paper from responsible sources FSC® C009448

The paper this book is printed on is certified against the Forest Stewardship Council® Standards. Griffin Press holds FSC chain of custody certification SGS-COC-005088. FSC promotes environmentally responsible, socially beneficial and economically viable management of the world's forests.

CONTENTS

Rule No. 1: Never lose money.
Rule No. 2: Never forget Rule No. 1.
- Warren Buffett

If saving money is wrong, I don't want to be right!
- William Shatner

This book contains all you need to become a bona fide Bill-Killer and save thousands of dollars over time, but to state the bleeding obvious . . . it's a book, not a financial advisor! So it can't give you personalised financial advice.

Any advice contained in this book is general in nature and doesn't take into account your particular objectives, personal circumstances or needs. If in doubt about your own situation you should seek appropriate advice.

Also, I've done my best to make sure all the information is up to date at the time of publication, but things do change quickly. So, where possible, I've also given you a website or other place where you can check the latest information at the time of reading.

One Big Switch is a registered business name of RevTech Media Pty Ltd (ABN 75 150 963 474), holder of an Australian Financial Services Licence (AFSL 455982) and an Australian Credit Licence (ACL 405918).

ABOUT THE AUTHOR

I'm that boring guy who talks about power prices at barbecues.

If you want to know who the cheapest electricity provider in south-east Queensland was in May last year for a four-person household with no solar panels, or which mobile provider has the best data limits this month, then I'm your guy.

But I never used to be this boring. In a former life I got 100 in my HSC, wrote jokes for *The Chaser* newspaper, had a monthly wine column in a glossy magazine, and worked at *The Sydney Morning Herald* for ten years, interviewing celebrities, pollies, crooks (and sometimes people who were all of the above).

I covered a coup in Fiji and the funeral of the Tongan King, dressed in a traditional Pacific man-skirt.

I probably knew less than you do about saving money and everything about spending it – and I *never* talked about household bills at barbecues.

I blame my job: I've been working at consumer clubs OneBigSwitch.com.au, FiftyUpClub.com and 9Saver.com.au for seven years now and we talk about bills all day long.

We've got over a million members around Australia and more than 1.4 million worldwide, and we use all that people power to negotiate special discounts on energy, insurance, home loans - or any other boring bill we can find.

Here's how we see it: we're boring so that *you* don't have to be!

You're welcome.

Apart from all sorts of arcane facts about electricity, insurance and petrol, being a money-saving nerd has taught me this about the war on household bills:

1. Life is too short to spend too much time thinking about bills (unless it's your job), but …
2. It's not hard to save thousands of dollars (as you'll see) once you know a few insider tricks, so …
3. If you don't spend just a few hours a year showing those bills who's boss, you're either made of money, or you're a mug!

As a dad of two kids aged seven and nine, I get it when people say they don't know where to start or they don't have the headspace for this stuff.

Who's got time between making the kids' lunches, dropping them at school, getting to work, earning a living, putting up with BS from your boss, caring for your ageing parents (or minding the grandkids so your kids can do all of the above), to research the cheapest electricity deal?

For most of us, life is too short to do it all the hard way.

So, don't. I've learnt a lot over the years about where to find the shortcuts to savings, and it's time to show you where they are.

That's what this book is for: to share some of the simple tricks we've learnt in eight years at Australia's biggest consumer network that will help you kill your household bills and never get ripped off again.

It's about making it easy to save over $1000 in an afternoon, and putting you in control again.

How do we know these tricks work? Because we use them ourselves and we see it every day among our million-plus members, who love to let us know when they've tracked down a saving.

No method is foolproof, but arm yourself with these weapons and you'll soon be the money-saving equivalent of Uma Thurman or Bruce Lee.

HOW TO USE THIS BOOK

Saving money is like fishing - you need some luck, but a bit of skill goes a long way.

Kill Bills! is a crash-course on 'fishing for savings' - it contains all the key insider tricks and local knowledge you need to catch the big ones.

But it's also a Bible of the major household bills to keep on the shelf and dip into any time you need to save on electricity, insurance, petrol, groceries and more.

Part 1 tells the story of how I saved over $3000 on my own bills in a year, the 'insider tricks' that helped me do it, and the other hacks that we've picked up in almost a decade of killing bills at One Big Switch.

I give you simple scripts you can use to get a better deal from your provider, and I also look at some basic human traits that can stop us from being Bill-Killers if we're not aware of them - things like 'loss aversion', 'status quo bias', 'choice paralysis' and Aussies' mortal fear of haggling!

Part 2 takes an in-depth look at nine of the major household bills, telling you what you need to know about the likes of electricity, insurance and broadband to make sure you can tackle them like a true Bill-Killer and never pay top dollar again.

You can read the book from start to finish and work your way up through the coloured Bill-Killing Belts if you want to become a full-blown kung fu master in the art of money-saving.

If you're in a hurry, no worries. There's a 'Quick Bill-Kill' in each chapter for those who want maximum results in the minimum time. If you follow this simple blow-by-blow plan for half a dozen bills in Part 4, you should be able to save over $1000 in an afternoon.

Otherwise, pick the book up when you receive your next big power bill or insurance renewal, go straight to the relevant chapter, and you'll find a simple rundown of what you can do about it.

And don't forget to tell us when you have a win! Tag us in a post on Facebook, Twitter or Instagram @OneBigSwitchAU and @KillBillsBook with the hashtag #KillBills.

That makes our day.

TRUE STORY: HOW I SAVED $3000 ON MY BILLS IN A YEAR (AND WHY IT WASN'T THAT HARD)

In the past year, I estimate I've saved a little over $3000 on my household bills, and it wasn't as hard as it might sound.

It didn't take me weeks of research and hours of wasted time waiting on the phone to foreign call centres - all I needed was a few hours, a stubborn refusal to be ripped off, and some insider tricks I've picked up in my day job, where I help Australian households to save on their bills.

Here's how I did it - and how you can too.

At the start of the year, I'm embarrassed to say that our home loan interest rate had risen by about 90 basis points (0.90%) before we'd really noticed.

Like thousands of Australians, it was because we had an 'interest-only' loan. Regulators have been clamping down on these riskier types of loans in recent years, so banks have been raising the rates on them. The Australian Competition and Consumer Commission estimated they made an extra $1 billion in interest from people like me who didn't immediately refinance.

I called our mortgage broker, Fawzi, and said we were happy to move to a 'principal and interest' loan for a lower rate, and what could he negotiate for us?

Fawzi called the bank. They offered a 0.60% reduction straight off the bat.

But I knew from experience that this was just their first offer.

I was also aware there were lenders out there offering variable rates with a '3' in front of them so I mentioned some of the examples I'd seen and I asked our broker to keep pushing. 'If we have to move, we'll move,' I said.

So he went back to the bank and played hardball. In the end they knocked off 0.80% p.a. And we got a big bank rate starting with a '3'. We've got decades left paying off our home, so that should add up to a small fortune over time.

Saving: About $2000 p.a.

We'd barely had time to celebrate that win when tragedy struck: our wi-fi went down.

I contacted our broadband provider and they said the local electricity network had replaced some poles and wires and accidentally cut the broadband cable for our area.

For the next couple of weeks, I hassled them for a date when it would be fixed, but they continued to blame the power company.

I busted the data cap on my mobile plan because we had no wi-fi at home. My kids nearly died of Netflix deprivation. We were forced to read books! It was like the 1980s all over again.

But then my wife told me she'd heard that if you lodge an official complaint with the telco ombudsman, the provider has to open a file and allocate someone to resolve your issue.

So I did. Two weeks later, the internet came back on. We'd been down for about a month but the telco contacted me to offer a $459.80 bill credit for the period (our plan costs $60 a month).

It was a huge inconvenience but at the end of the day we chalked it up as a win - about six months' free wi-fi in exchange for a month without it.

Saving: About $460

In the middle of the year, I chopped up my credit card.

Like most Australians, I've had about $3000 debt on a card for the past decade. Sometimes it was more, sometimes less, but like a yo-yo dieter, I always ended up back at about $3000 somehow.

Also like a lot of Australians, we had some savings sitting in another account, reducing the cost of our mortgage payments (an 'offset').

But this made no sense: I was paying 20% p.a. interest on my $3000 credit card debt while our savings were working to reduce the interest on my mortgage, where the rate was less than a quarter of that.

I decided to bite the bullet (once again, thanks to some encouragement from my wiser, better half), pay the card off and chop it up.

This will save me about $600 a year in interest. Sure, I was getting points and it was handy to have, but I'd rather be debt-free, and I've now got a debit card that I can use anywhere a credit card is welcome.

Saving: About $600 p.a.

I was on a pretty good mobile deal with amaysim, getting 10GB of data for $40 a month. But I know from dealing with telcos that the mobile market changes faster than just about any other household bill.

As the data becomes cheaper for the providers, there's a sort of 'data creep' that occurs. Every year or so, the telcos give a big boost to all their new plans - and once one does it, the others have to follow.

So when I saw my provider Optus offering 30GB for $35 on their website, I checked whether I was out of contract and - bingo! - I upgraded.

All I had to do to get more data for less was to re-contract for another 12 months. Fine with me.

Saving: About $60 p.a.

Finally, it was time to check my energy plan. I was on an 18% electricity discount with very low rates, so overall it used to be one of the cheapest around.

But surprise, surprise - sometime in the past year my provider had rejigged their offer so I was now getting only 12% pay-on-time discount unless I pre-purchased about $400 of power at a time.

Most energy plans in Australia work like this - the retailer can change them at any point in time as long as they send you an FYI (which is sometimes buried in the fine print of your next bill).

So it was time to switch, and I knew that One Big Switch had an enormous 30% pay-on-time discount available from Alinta Energy in NSW, so that was an easy decision. When my gas provider, AGL, heard I was leaving, they offered me 32% off electricity too if I stayed, so I switched yet again.

Saving: About $150 p.a.

So there it is - about $3270 worth of savings over the year from just a few hours of haggling, complaining, switching and, yes, listening to my wife.

If someone offered you over $3000 for a few hours work, wouldn't you take it? (You would. Even if it meant listening to your partner!)

To make the savings above, I used five of the insider tricks I've learnt in my years at One Big Switch:

- the De Niro;
- the Under-the-Table Deal;
- the Squeaky Wheel;
- the Moving Target; and
- the Good Listener.

Read on to understand how each of these tricks works, how you can use them too, and a few other tidbits of inside info I've picked up that could save you thousands.

But first! Just in case you think you need to be an expert to get a result like this, below is the story of 'super-switcher' Leanne, who in just one afternoon achieved one of the biggest wins I've ever seen in the battle against household bills.

True Story: Leanne the super-switcher saves $3749

Leanne from Sydney's inner-west is a single mum with a high-powered job in IT.

She's time-poor, but she put aside one afternoon and went on the equivalent of a money-saving lucky streak, achieving the best results I've ever seen in the battle against household bills.

Leanne killed five different household bills in one afternoon and estimated afterwards that she saved:

- $610 a year on health insurance;
- $1595 a year on home and contents insurance;
- $777 a year on car insurance; and
- $333 a year on two mobile phones.

She also did a 'De Niro' on her energy provider, telling them she'd been offered a great discount elsewhere and was ready to walk.

So they matched the offer she'd found, saving her an estimated $433 in the coming year on energy.

Add up the numbers and weep.

'I saved $3749, and it took me two hours to do it,' Leanne told 7 News.

'I'm really tired of these vendors who take you for granted . . . I think we all need to just get more confident and switch!'

I asked her what her advice was to anyone who's ready to have a go.

'Just put aside the time, have the paperwork in front of you so you're prepared for the conversation and you're not fluffing around on the phone. Be confident but polite. Ask to speak to a manager.

'And I think it's best to focus on the big ticket items, particularly the annuity bills that come in every few months or every year like energy and insurance.

'Energy is the hard one because you've got to look at the back page and compare all the rates as well as the discounts. But it is possible to save a lot of money, and sometimes you don't even need to switch to do it.'

PART 1

THE 9 INSIDER TRICKS YOU NEED TO WIN THE WAR ON HOUSEHOLD BILLS

HOW TO USE PART 1 OF THIS BOOK

In this first part of the book, I'll run through nine of the insider tricks I've come across in almost a decade of helping people to save money on their bills.

They range from the 'De Niro' to the 'Mystery-Shopper', from the 'Elizabeth Taylor' to the 'Red Dog'. I've given them new names but these bill-killing strategies are common knowledge to those who work in the energy, insurance or home loan industries - but unknown to most of us who don't. They're also the hacks I've tested myself and seen our members use to save hundreds or sometimes thousands of dollars.

Master them all, Grasshopper, and your household bills will quiver with fear from the moment they land in your letterbox!

CHAPTER 1
THE DE NIRO

This trick might just be the most important one in the book so I've made it #1.

I've also named it after one of my favourite movies – the 1995 Michael Mann gangster flick *Heat*.

In *Heat*, Robert De Niro plays Neil McCauley, a professional thief who never gets caught because – just like a shark – he never stops moving.

The movie gets its name from his most famous piece of advice:

> "*Don't let yourself get attached to anything you are not willing to walk out on in 30 seconds flat if you feel the heat around the corner.*"

McCauley then disappears as the police close in, leaving his poor girlfriend behind!

While I can't condone the treatment of his girlfriend, I most certainly do recommend his attitude if you're determined to pay as little as possible for your bills.

If you're not willing to walk away, if you're not ruthlessly mobile, you'll never get the best deals and sooner or later you'll end up getting ripped off.

Many times you won't need to move at all! But just being prepared to switch providers will show you're serious about saving. It puts you in a completely different class of customer – a group that businesses call the 'Price-Chasers'.

Businesses know they have to work that little bit harder to win over the Price-Chasers – so they often do.

True Story: From Richard Wilkins to Lisa Wilkinson and Russell from Queensland, the 'De Niro' is a winner

When Channel Nine entertainment guru Richard Wilkins told me he had a shocker of a power bill, I suggested I introduce him to the De Niro.

Dickie's probably met the real De Niro, but in this case I meant the money-saving trick, not the two-time Oscar winner.

So we called his power company and asked them to please explain why, as a longstanding loyal customer, Dickie was only receiving a 4% discount.

They offered to increase it to a 26% pay-on-time discount on the spot, but we explained that he'd been offered a massive 42% pay-on-time discount through the consumer club 9Saver.com.au (entirely true).

So they put us through to the retention team, who increased the offer to 28% guaranteed discount and a free smart meter (worth about $200), which was good enough to keep him – for now.

Fellow TV star Lisa Wilkinson also knows the value of the De Niro. On Channel Ten's *The Project*, she said she'd been looking at switching through a 'group-buying syndicate' (maybe the one where I work, but I don't know for sure) until she got a call from her retailer at the last moment.

'[My electricity company] said, "We're going to give you a 15% discount!"'

But Lisa told them, 'You know what? I'm still going to call that buying group.'

So, 'They called again and came back with an offer of 18%.

'In the end, I ended up with 28% discount, and all because I just kept saying no,' Lisa said.

Russell, a One Big Switch member from

Queensland, isn't quite as famous as Richard or Lisa but he plays just as tough – and proves you don't need to be a big name to achieve a big result.

'Although I did not take up the offer [from One Big Switch],' he wrote to me, 'I used the offer to negotiate a better deal with my current supplier.

'I have done this on every occasion you have had an Energy Switch campaign. I also did this with the Health Insurance campaign.

'Just wanted to let you know that although I haven't taken up the winning offers, I still obtained better deals. Keep up the good work!'

Same to you, Russ!

I used the 'De Niro' myself earlier in the book to save $2000 p.a. on our mortgage. It was only when we let our bank know that we'd seen lower interest rates out there and we were prepared to move that they came back with their best offer.

The essence of the 'De Niro' is leverage. (As Lord Nelson once said, 'A fleet of British ships of war are the best negotiators in Europe.') So before you can threaten to leave, you've got to have leverage – and the best leverage is to have in your hand a really good offer from another provider.

If your current provider can match it, you can stay. If they can't, or won't match it, you can switch.

Either way, you win.

Here's a basic script to use when you call your provider up:

> *'Hi there, my name is [Robert De Niro/ Richard Wilkins/Lisa Wilkinson/Russell from Queensland]. I've been a loyal customer of yours for _______ years and I'd like to stay on, but I've just received a really good offer from another provider and I think it might be a better deal than the one I'm on. _______ has offered me _______ . I wondered whether you can match it or even beat it? If you can, I'll lock it in right now. Perhaps you could put me through to someone on your retention team to see if they can help.'*

Are you a 'Price-Chaser' or a 'Sleeping Beauty'?

Report after report has found that loyalty is all but dead when it comes to household bills. It's the customers they call 'Price-Chasers', those who are *most* prepared to move, who usually get the best deals.

Take power prices, for example. The Australian Competition and Consumer Commission (ACCC) spent a year looking into why our power prices are some of the highest in the world and concluded this:

> "*Those customers who have been active in the market, regularly reviewing options and switching*

between offers ... are likely paying less than the average cost to retailers of supplying electricity.”

(Translation: power companies are *losing* money on the customers who regularly move plans or providers!)

There's a saying in some businesses that it doesn't pay 'to wake the Sleeping Beauty'.

The 'Sleeping Beauty' is a longstanding, loyal customer who never reads a book like this one, never asks for a better deal and never, ever leaves. The only way businesses can afford to cover the cost of attracting the 'Price-Chasers' above is to make extra margin out of the older, more loyal customers, these so-called 'Sleeping Beauties'.

This cross-subsidy is the backbone of whole industries, from energy to insurance and home loans. It's not fair but it's the way of the world.

The charity St Vincent de Paul, better known as

Vinnies, takes an annual look at the difference between what Price-Chasers pay for electricity, by shopping around for the cheapest offers on the market, compared to Sleeping Beauties, who end up on the most expensive 'standing offers'.

In 2018, the gap reached as much as $2675 a year for two hypothetical Victorian households using the same amount of energy! In other states it was not so big, but still around $1000. That's an enormous 'Loyalty Tax' to pay, just for doing nothing.

Insurance is often the same. As I explain later, former consumer watchdog Allan Fels has undertaken research that estimates the old, loyal 'Sleeping Beauty' customers pay 34% more than the new Price-Chaser customers for home insurance.

So if you're a Sleeping Beauty, you need to understand that you're paying extra while you slumber so that all the De Niros out there can score great deal after great deal (or steal after steal!).

CHAPTER 2
THE UNDER-THE-TABLE DEAL

Contrary to what a lot of consumer advocates tell you, most businesses aren't inherently bad. They're not trying to screw you at every possible opportunity.

Businesses are not immoral; if anything, they're 'amoral'. They're like machines or robots that are programmed to provide a service in exchange for money. They're motivated by profit, of course, but not by malice.

But the thing about a robot is this: if you know how the machine works, you can usually beat it at its own game.

I remember learning a vital lesson about prices as a kid. I grew up around the snowfields on the

NSW/Victoria border and my childhood hero was my dad's best mate Walter, a big, Swiss mountain of a bloke.

Like a lot of our family friends, Walter worked at one of the ski resorts, and one day I asked him how they set the price of a lift ticket.

'They charge $50,' he explained in his matter-of-fact Swiss way, 'because if they charge $60, the mountain isn't full. And if they charge $40, it's too full.'

I was dumbfounded. I always assumed they set the price as low as they could, to compete with other resorts.

I thought it was a case of 'lift ticket = cost of providing service + small margin'.

But no – they charged *as much* as they could without driving people away.

It was actually 'lift ticket = cost of providing service + maximum margin possible without empty mountain'.

As a grown-up, I can now see it makes perfect sense. Businesses will charge you what you're prepared to pay.

This drives people *crazy*. Why should we have to ask for their best deal? Why don't we get rewarded for loyalty? This is BS!

All of which is true. But look at it the other way around: here we are, trying to work out how to pay *them* as little as possible for their services. So we're playing the game too. And if you're reading this book, you're finally playing to win.

Most businesses have several offers:

1. Their Base Offer, for anyone silly enough to take it. This one makes them the most money, so they dangle it out there just in case.
2. Their On-Market Offer, for those who ask for something better, but don't push them all the way.
3. Their Under-the-Table Offer, for those customers they really need to work hard to keep.

How do you get the Under-the-Table offers? Once again, you need leverage, and there are a couple of ways to get yourself some of that.

You can threaten to leave, which often leads to your provider making you a so-called 'retention offer'.

Some big businesses have whole teams who *just* work on 'retention'. When they hear you're leaving, they will put you through to the 'retention team' or you'll get a barrage of calls from them. Pick up the phone! That's when you know you're about to be made an offer that's very, very hard to refuse!

But of course, it pays to have a Plan B before you make that threat.

So first, use brokers, comparison sites and buying groups like One Big Switch to find an alternative offer that gives you leverage. One Big Switch has a million-plus members and we use that to unlock special group discounts. Motoring clubs, footy clubs and other groups sometimes do similar negotiations. There's plenty of help out there.

True Story: My mate Mutchy gets a 30% discount, just by asking

I was having a few quiet beers with my mate Mutchy one night and I asked him what energy deal he was on. He said he was getting a 20% discount.

I'd heard from some of our members that his provider had been offering a 30% discount under the table to try and keep some customers who planned to leave.

So we harnessed our Dutch courage and rang and told them we'd seen a 30% discount from another provider available via One Big Switch (also true), and they matched it on the spot.

All up, it took about five minutes on the phone and saved him a couple of hundred dollars a year.

So I made him pay for the beers.

Why Aussies don't like to haggle

It's not you. It's us. It's a cultural thing. Most Australians just find haggling difficult.

The travel Bible *Lonely Planet* tells foreign visitors that 'Haggling isn't part of Australia's commercial culture', so don't bother.

According to a 2017 survey of 1700 people around the world, Aussies placed ninth out of 16 countries for 'enjoying' a haggle, and a lowly 15th out of 16 for the results we get - partly because our shops and service providers don't often encourage it.

> *"Less than half of Australians enjoyed negotiating for lower prices, although they typically achieved 15% off when they did."*

These days we do haggle a bit for cars, for furniture and whitegoods and that sort of thing, because we've become used to The Good Guys, Harvey Norman and Bing Lee encouraging it.

We might go back and forth a bit with someone in the Trading Post or on Gumtree. *'Tell 'im he's dreaming!'* But compared to somewhere like Asia, it's culturally just not as ingrained in us.

In 2013, researchers surveyed over 200 Chinese and Australian negotiators about their haggling 'tricks' for the *Journal of Business Ethics*.

They ran them through the 36 classic tactics outlined in an ancient Chinese essay on strategy, called *The Secret Art of War: The 36 Stratagems*.

They found Aussies were more comfortable feigning negative feelings or emotions in a negotiation, or using threats to win!

But the Chinese were more comfortable with most of the stratagems - and therefore presumably more comfortable with using haggling and negotiating tricks in general.

Namely, the Chinese negotiators were more comfortable feigning positive feelings, diverting attention, misrepresenting information, making false or insincere promises, or withholding information to win.

This fits well with the impressions of Aussie travel writer Ben Groundwater, who believes there's a word for people like him who find haggling a real chore: they're called 'Westerners'!

> "*We're just not built for this game. You never have to haggle over anything in the Western world ... The shopping experience for us is a cut-and-dried game. There's a price: you either pay it or you don't.*"

So if the thought of asking your power or insurance company for a better deal makes you feel awkward, you're not Robinson Crusoe. You're quite typical.

But once you've tried it and had a win, once you know who to haggle with and what to say, I think you'll find that haggling is kind of addictive.

Take the tip from JFK, who famously said: *'Let us never negotiate out of fear. But let us never fear to negotiate.'*

Once you get a sense of the power you have as a customer – a power we all have but maybe don't realise or exercise fully – there really is no stopping you.

CHAPTER 3
THE MYSTERY-SHOPPER

When I was a uni student, my mate Cal called me to say he'd found the perfect uni job.

'All you have to do,' he said, in utter disbelief, 'is go shopping! And then you just write a report on how lousy the staff were, and they pay you!'

They're called 'mystery-shoppers', and businesses use these undercover agents to check up on their own employees and franchisees.

Pretty dastardly trick, hey? Well, real customers can use this one to kill household bills, too. Here's how.

Most businesses put their prices up every year, to cover inflation and increases in their costs. But some businesses also put their prices up to make more money out of you, even if their costs haven't risen by that much - mainly because they think they can get away with it. They call this their 'back book' strategy, or 'increasing their margin'.

INSIDE INFO: Research by the NSW Insurance Levy Monitor has found that some sophisticated companies employ teams of highly skilled actuaries to create algorithms that predict precisely how much they can increase your price before you'll leave them.

That same report found that existing customers who renew their home insurance pay on average 34% more than new customers. They also found that 'quotes range from say $1000 to $2700 for the same house and contents' from different providers.

That's a big fat tax on loyal customers!

But it creates a loophole for those in the know.

How do you exploit this loophole? It's time to don your disguise and go mystery-shopping!

How to do a Mystery-Shop

1. Put on some dark glasses and a fake moustache, Groucho Marx-style.
2. Go to your provider's website.
3. Enter the same details as your current deal or policy, eg '$500,000 of home and contents cover on a three-bedroom freestanding house, built in 1960' etc. (Tip: these details should be on your renewal notice if you need to check them.)
4. But don't use the same name or address. This is because they will have yours stored already. Instead, use a different name (such as your partner's) and a different address in the same postcode (such as your neighbour's, where the risk profile of the suburb should be identical).
5. See what price they quote you. If it's the same as your current price, you're on a winner! Renew your policy and spend the rest of the day at the beach.
6. But if it's radically lower than your own price, ask them to 'please explain'! When faced with your research, most businesses will negotiate to keep you. If they don't, maybe it's time to get a quote from another website ...

Once again, here's a basic script to use when you've done a Mystery-Shop:

> *"Hi, my name's [Groucho Marx/Robert De Niro/Insert real name here] and I've been a loyal customer of yours for ______ years. I've recently received my renewal notice. I couldn't help noticing that it's gone up by _____. And I also couldn't help noticing that it's ______ more than you're charging a new customer with similar details to me. I know this because I got a quote on your website for a new policy with my details and I must have accidentally put my neighbour's address in. Whoops! Anyhow, the quote came in at _____. How is that fair? I'd like you to match that new customer price please, and if you can I'll renew right now. If you can't, I've got a quote from another provider and I'm tempted to take my business elsewhere."*

If you don't get the result you're after at first, ask to speak to their manager! (More on that in Chapter 7, 'The Squeaky Wheel'.)

What is 'anchoring'? And how can you use this classic marketing tactic to kill your own bills?

Almost 50 years ago, two Israeli psychologists identified a number of classic consumer habits in a series of experiments that ended up winning them the Nobel Prize.

Daniel Kahneman and Amos Tversky called these habits our 'systematic biases'. They went on to become known as the pioneers of behavioural economics, which now influences how businesses sell us stuff, how governments convince us to do stuff, and (from this point on) how you and I resist being manipulated by those businesses and governments.

One of the biases or habits they identified was called 'anchoring' and it's behind a lot of the marketing and political campaigning that's targeted at us every single day of our lives.

'How much would you expect to pay for this robot vacuum cleaner?' asks the guy in the late night infomercial.

'$2000? $1000? No! It's yours for just four easy instalments of $199.99!'

Why does he start with a question you've never really asked yourself, and then answer it for you before you've had a chance to think about it, like Kevin Rudd?

He's dropping an 'anchor' for you with the higher prices, of course, which he hopes will set your expectation. And then he's undercutting it with the real price, to make it seem cheap.

On price tags and stickers, you see it all the time. 'Recommended Retail Price: $35. Our Price: $25!'

They're giving you the regular price as an anchor to make their price seem more attractive by comparison.

Experienced negotiators use anchoring all the time. They'll start with an 'ambit claim' or a borderline-outrageous request in a bid to anchor expectations. They hope this then gives them a better chance of achieving their real aim, which is less ambitious.

'My client deserves a $50,000 pay rise.'

'Your client can have $10,000.'

'How about $15,000?'

'Deal!'

Even charities do it. When they ask, 'How much would you like to donate? $50, $100 or $500?', they're 'anchoring' you to think that $50 is the norm, or the starting point, because research and experience shows the average donation will be higher this way than if they gave options starting at, say, $20.

Human beings need these anchors. They put the 'educated' in our 'educated guesses'. If someone doesn't give them to us, we find our own.

But knowledge is power, of course, and now that you understand how anchoring works, you too can enlist it in the war on bills. Here's how.

Anchoring is a vital element in employing 'The De Niro' or in accessing 'Under-the-Table Deals', for starters. As I said earlier, your best chance of getting one of these deals is when you've already got another good offer to use as leverage. That other offer is your 'anchor'.

When you tell your provider, 'I've just been offered a 30% discount on my electricity' or 'I can get sports on Kayo for only $25 a month, so why would I keep paying over $100 for Foxtel?', you've just given *them* an anchor.

They now know where the psychological starting point is to try to win you over.

Anchoring is also vital in the 'Mystery-Shopper' trick I've just described. Your mystery-shopping expedition creates an alternative quote.

Even if it's not a 100% real quote (because you've used your neighbour's address details, for example), it becomes a very real anchor for your insurer.

It's one of *their* quotes, and that makes it pretty hard to argue against. So they will often try to match it or compromise with you if they can.

And in most cases, the best way to find a good 'anchor' for your negotiation is to be internet-savvy, which we'll talk about in Chapter 8, 'David's Slingshot'.

CHAPTER 4
THE ELIZABETH TAYLOR

'Your energy plan will be renewed, Joel,' said the letter I received a few years back from my electricity provider.

But the fine print revealed they'd 'renewed' me on a discount 10% lower than I had the previous year. How kind!

Needless to say, they're now my ex-provider. But this is a common story, especially when it comes to power and insurance companies. Entire industries have been built on this 'Honeymoon' model.

In business it's known as a 'front book versus back book pricing strategy', where your 'front book' is made up of those new customers who receive attractive joining offers (remember the 'Price-Chasers' from

Chapter 1?), while your 'back book' is full of all those 'Sleeping Beauties' on old prices or rising prices who kindly pay extra to help fund the newbies.

I call it 'the Honeymoon Strategy' and from a customer's point of view it looks like this:

1. First, they give you a very cheap one-year offer to win you over (sometimes they're even prepared to lose money on you in the first year if that's what it takes).
2. Then, they quietly wind back your discount, or increase your rate or premium. And because of our human traits of 'Status Quo Bias' and 'Loss Aversion', which I'll explain later, they take a punt that you'll be too busy or too lazy or too afraid of change to dump them.
3. Finally, they make their money out of you in years two, three and four - provided your natural aversion to change still proves strong enough to stop you from switching or complaining.

Companies do this because it works: extensive testing and experience have shown it time and time again. Most of us don't want to shop around or move providers every year. Who has time and energy for that, right?!

But that's the insider trick here: the 'Honeymoon Strategy' of businesses actually creates a loophole for Bill-Killers. If you're prepared to move regularly, you can win and win again from this business model.

You can see where I'm going here. The way to pay as little as possible for your power bills and a range of other bills too is to adopt the 'Elizabeth Taylor' approach and take honeymoon after honeymoon after honeymoon.

You can honeymoon with different providers and sometimes even with the same provider more than once (hello again, Richard Burton!).

And sometimes you don't even have to leave to get a second honeymoon - when your plan goes up in the second year and you call the provider and say 'Please explain', they will often bring it back down and give you another 'Price-Chaser' deal to stay.

So don't end up in an unhappy marriage with your providers. There are plenty of other fish in the sea. Switch or negotiate a better offer if you see your price rise suddenly.

After all, not shopping around every year or two can be very costly. Just look at a typical power bill, for example. Let's say you're on a great one-year electricity discount of 25 per cent.

After 12 months, it reverts to zero discount, which is common. The company might send you a letter, as they're required to do now (but not in the past), but maybe you miss it or you just don't get around to doing anything about it for whatever reason (also a common situation).

In the next year, that lost discount could mean your plan costs you over $1000 more than the year before.

The good people of St Vincent de Paul are so worried about this phenomenon that they do an annual report showing how big the gap is between the best discounted 'honeymoon' offer and the worst zero discount 'old married couple' offer (my words, not theirs).

As I mentioned earlier, in 2018 their report showed the gap was up to:

- $240 for electricity in the ACT;
- $1040 for electricity in NSW;
- $600 for electricity in south-east Qld;
- $1165 for electricity in SA; and
- $2675 for electricity in Victoria!

This gap should now shrink thanks to some major changes to the energy market in mid-2019, but you get the idea.

The gap between the honeymooners and the 'Sleeping Beauties' can be either a danger or an opportunity. It's up to you.

True Story: Bek Saves $769 after she was downgraded without realising

Journalist Bek Day is a self-taught expert on health insurance savings (you can see some of her top hacks in Chapter 13). But she hadn't looked closely at her energy bill for a year or two.

When she got involved in an energy campaign we were running, she interrogated her latest bill

and found she'd been downgraded to a plan with no discount. This is more common than you'd think.

In Australia, most energy discounts last for a year or two and you are then downgraded - unless you pick another plan.

Bek switched providers and took up a 30% discount for two years and our energy analyst estimated it would save her $769 in the first year.

'I was absolutely stoked,' she told the *Today Show*, 'and to be honest, it was only when I got a really eye-wateringly high power bill that I decided to finally take my own advice, bite the bullet and call up and make the switch.

'Like a lot of Aussies, I found out I was on a dud deal. So that's an extra nearly $800 in my pocket.'

CHAPTER 5

THE MOVING TARGET

Do you know what the hardest thing is about winning the war on bills?

Bills don't stand still!

You can switch your electricity plan but the following July the rates increase by 15% and suddenly you're not on the best plan anymore.

You can sign up for a killer home loan rate but then your bank raises it by 100 basis points, or you find a great insurance offer that saves you a packet but come your next renewal, your premium jumps by $200.

Each bill is a moving target and you can win battle after battle but the war is never really over.

But here's the thing: the 'Moving Target' creates another opportunity for you to save money.

Why? Because each time the market changes, there's a chance you can get a better deal for your dosh than you had before.

The key here is to identify markets where prices are *dropping*. In those examples, if you move plans every year, you'll find you get better and better bang for the same buck.

But set and forget, on the other hand, and you'll end up marooned on an old pricing tier and paying too much - like that feeling when you buy a new TV and you see a bigger, better model at a lower price a month later.

Right now, the best examples of household bills where prices are *dropping* are mobile and broadband - because the technology is moving so fast.

Consider this: it used to be common for people to pay $100 a month for mobile or broadband plans with not much data.

Now, it's common to see plans for $60 a month with unlimited data (for broadband) or about $40 a month for 30 Gigabytes of data (for mobile - that's enough to watch about 40 SD episodes of *Game of Thrones*).

This is happening for two reasons: one, we are using so much more data every year, and two, the cost of data is dropping for the providers.

In the three months leading up to June 2018, for example, Aussies downloaded 3.8 million terabytes.

Seven years ago, we only downloaded about 7% of that amount over the same time period!

We're now downloading or streaming about 14 times the data we downloaded seven years ago.

But in 2011, did an internet plan or a mobile plan cost any less than it does today? Not really. NBN plans now cost about $60–$100 a month, which was roughly what we paid for dial-up internet in the early days.

The graph below from the Australian Bureau of Statistics is one of those pictures that's worth a thousand words. It shows how our downloads have skyrocketed.

This target moves very quickly and you have to ride the rocket!

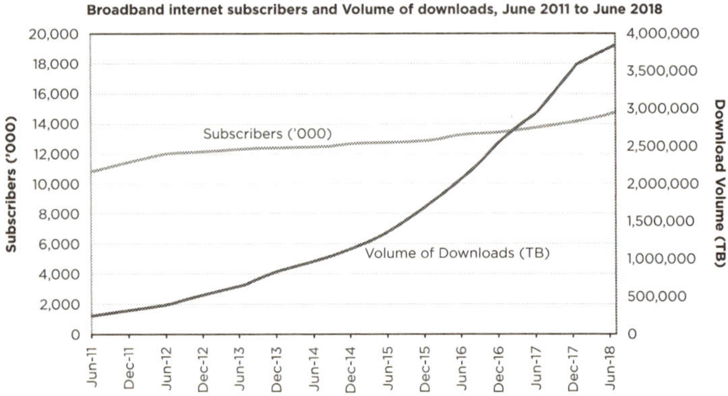

Source: ABS

True Story: How my first telco learnt a thing or two from the Hare Krishnas

My first ever ADSL broadband plan had a 300GB download limit. Not long after I signed up, the provider (iiNet) contacted me to say they'd upgraded us to a 1000GB download limit.

I nearly fell out of my chair. There must be some mistake, I thought. Who gives anyone anything for free these days, apart from the Hare Krishnas?

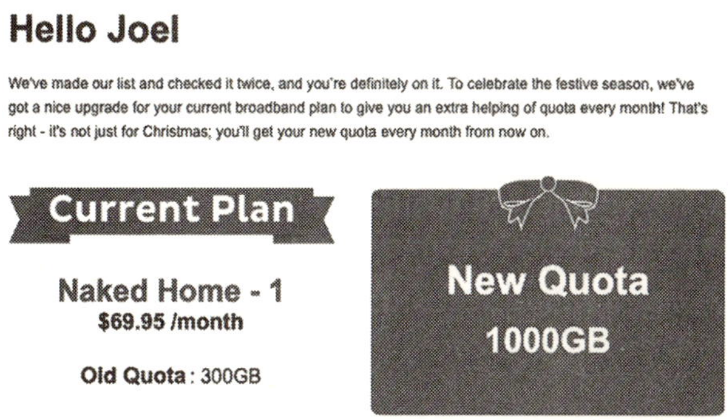

But my telco had in fact borrowed an age-old trick pioneered by that brightly robed, shaven-haired, chanting crew from the International Society for Krishna Consciousness.

The Hare Krishnas have long had a successful fundraising technique that involves giving out flowers and then asking for a donation. Most people take the gift, and then find it hard to say no when asked for a few bucks.

This trick was so effective that the state of California ended up banning them from airports!

What's that got to do with my old telco? Well, they locked me in for years with that gift. They bought my loyalty.

What I didn't realise at the time was that it cost them virtually nothing. The extra data was a gift of sorts (they didn't have to give it to us) but the data was costing them less and less each day so it cost them no more to give us more.

Moral of this story? Telcos should periodically give us more for the same price (and if they don't, we should change plans regularly).

Oh, and more businesses should give their customers gifts! They might find we're more loyal if they show us some loyalty first.

Why 'good enough' is almost always good enough: 'Satisficers' versus 'Maximisers'

At this point, I think it's important to let you off the hook.

In this book I want to demonstrate how to really show your bills who's boss, with minimal time and effort. What I *don't* want to do is make you feel guilty if you're not always on the absolute best option.

You don't *have* to switch every bill every year. You don't *always* have to get the best under-the-table deal. You don't have to move *every* time the telco market does. Who's got time for all that? Life is short, after all.

These are general principles and the important thing is that you know them and you do these things from time to time. But don't be too hard on yourself.

It's bizarre but sometimes being a perfectionist can lead to doing nothing at all.

American psychologist Barry Schwartz really hit this nail on the head in the noughties when he told people:

> "*'Good enough' is almost always good enough.*"

In his bestselling book *The Paradox of Choice: Why More is Less*, Schwartz's research found you're actually more likely to be happy in life if you're what he called a 'satisficer'. 'Satisficers' are happy to settle for 'good enough'.

'Maximizers', on the other hand, who always have to find the absolute *best* or *cheapest* option, are less satisfied with their lives. (They do earn more, mind you, but they're also more likely to regret their decisions, and to be depressed.)

It used to be that there was only one government-owned energy or telco provider (there still is in some parts of Australia). A lot of us are very nostalgic for those days: why do we have to chase down a better energy or mobile deal? Why have we created all this work for ourselves?

Schwartz says we've created so many choices in our modern lives that it can confuse us and make us miserable. In one famous study, psychologists presented 24 different types of jam to shoppers and gave them a voucher for $1 off a jar. But they bought less jam than another group of shoppers who were presented with just six options.

'Unconstrained choice,' he says, 'is paralyzing, not liberating', and he has a point.

Let's say you need to choose a laptop from the thousands of options now available to us. His tip is:

> “*Whenever you need a new laptop, call up one of your maximizer friends and say, 'What laptop did you buy?' And you buy that laptop. Is it going to be the perfect laptop for you? Probably not. Is it going to be a good enough laptop for you? Absolutely. It takes you five minutes to make a decision instead of five weeks and it's a 'good enough' decision.*
>
> *I don't think you can delegate all of the decisions in life in this way but you can certainly delegate a hell of a lot of them. What's best for your friend won't be best for you but chances are it will be good enough for you.*”

There's no need to be on top of every bill *all* the time. I'm certainly not.

Just don't let yourself do the opposite, which is nothing. The biggest mistake we can make when it comes to our bills is to do nothing at all. Hopefully this book will show how even a small effort can produce big savings.

Which brings us to the next trick you need to master: listening . . .

CHAPTER 6
THE GOOD LISTENER

This next trick's not rocket science.

Sometimes, all you have to do to save hundreds or thousands of dollars is to ask around. People love to tell you when they've killed a bill, and they're unlikely to recommend something that hasn't worked out for them.

'Word of mouth' is the #1 most trusted source of information when we make purchasing decisions, according to the *Nielsen Global Trust in Advertising Survey*.

It's almost twice as trusted as the material you read: 92% of us trust recommendations from friends, followed by 70% trusting online reviews and 58% trusting editorials or articles.

The management consultants at McKinsey believe that word of mouth plays a role in up to 50% of all purchasing decisions, and is *twice* as powerful as paid advertising.

So the first thing we should do when we want to save on insurance or energy or our home loan is ask around.

And it works: people close to you will feel like they own the result of their recommendations, so they're unlikely to tip you into a deal that's no good (unless they don't realise it yet).

And someone you know might actually be something of an expert on that particular bill - so tapping into your network is a no-brainer.

There are a few different ways that being a 'Good Listener' can save you big bucks over time.

Ask an expert

Obviously, if you know someone who works in the banking, energy or insurance industry, or just has some inside knowledge, go there first.

As I hope this book shows, a bit of inside info can prove priceless.

Friends regularly ask me what the best energy offer is, for example. It changes every month, and it all depends what you need, so the answer is never straightforward.

But I love being able to help them out, and over the years I've upgraded my dad from zero discount to 28%

off his electricity with the same provider using a One Big Switch special deal, I've helped another friend get 30% off because I knew *his* provider was offering it as an 'under-the-table deal', and I've helped a couple of celebs with big power bills to slash over $1000 per annum from their bills - just because it came up in conversation while I was on set for a TV segment.

These days, there are quite sophisticated comparison sites for most household bills too, so you can get a really quick sense of what's available (except for those 'under-the-table deals', of course).

Ask your 'friends'

Social media isn't just good for posting selfies and cat videos. It's also a great way to tap the so-called 'hive mind' or the 'wisdom of the crowd'.

Ask a question like 'Where's the best coffee in Melbourne?' or 'Top ten albums of all time?' on Facebook and you'll almost break the internet.

But I've found you also get a great result when you ask for people's money-saving tips.

So why not use that collective wisdom to solve problems like 'What's a good broadband deal at the moment?' or 'Anyone got any tips for getting my power bill down?"

We're all in this war on bills together and people love to work together to even the playing field with these large, sophisticated businesses that provide our power or insurance or wifi. In Chapter 18, you'll see how I asked my Facebook friends if anyone has recently saved thousands by getting a better deal on their mortgage, and within 24 hours I had half a dozen great leads to follow up.

Online reviews

You can also take the tips of strangers. At websites such as www.productreview.com.au, www.ozbargain.com.au and www.choice.com.au, a mixture of experts and amateurs give their views on all sorts of products, including most household bills.

These can be a useful touchpoint - particularly when the reviews are by experts (as in the case of CHOICE, which is why you have to pay for them) or by complete amateurs on a non-profit basis (as in the case of Ozbargain, which is a large and very quirky online community of hardcore Bill-Killers who even swap notes about KFC specials they've seen!).

But you should take some online review sites with a grain of salt. Your electricity provider has bad reviews? Check out some other electricity providers' reviews before you jump to too many conclusions - you'll find they almost *all* have bad reviews. (People just don't like electricity companies. They've even been compared to cigarette companies in recent reputational research, which I think is a bit rough.)

INSIDE INFO: Some review sites are also being gamed. Any business that cares enough about online reviews will have people working behind the scenes on generating positive reviews, so the best-reviewed providers are sometimes just the best-resourced. In fact, the way some of these sites make a buck is by going to businesses and saying 'we can help you improve your reviews for a fee'. So don't believe everything you read online (as if I needed to tell you that)!

CHAPTER 7 THE SQUEAKY WHEEL

As the old saying goes, 'The squeaky wheel gets the oil', and unfortunately it's often true.

If you don't ask for a better deal, and you don't officially complain when things go wrong, you're unlikely to get the best possible results.

This doesn't mean you have to be a serial complainant, forever firing off cranky emails (believe me, there are plenty of those 'trolls' out there, but they put *way* too much time into their whingeing).

What it does mean is that if you want to get a result from a large company with thousands of customers, you need to master the art of 'the Squeaky Wheel' and learn to 'whinge well'.

There are three escalating steps to being an effective whinger: whingeing to the boss, whingeing in public, and whingeing to the regulator.

Each time you try one and don't get a result, you should take it to the next step.

STEP #1: Whinge to the boss

The trick to the 'Squeaky Wheel' is to get your complaint noticed by someone as high on the tree as you possibly can.

Your complaint is like one of those little penguins in the David Attenborough docos, competing with hundreds of other penguins to climb out of the roiling ocean without being dashed against the rocks before it can make it to the front of the queue.

As a manager who sometimes has to take calls about people's complaints, I can't believe I'm telling you this. But the fact is that if one of our million-plus members has an issue at One Big Switch and they get through to me, they've got a better chance of a rapid resolution.

Why? I usually take personal responsibility for the case and I ask my team to help me resolve it ASAP. I don't see a lot of these cases, unlike the member services team who deal with inquiries all day, so the ones I see do stand out to me.

Big businesses are the same, but multiplied by a hundred.

With them, you really need to make your penguin stand out somehow!

So if you complain and you don't get a fair result immediately, ask for it to be escalated to a manager and tell them why you think it's unfair.

A Telstra customer told me she once wrote directly to the CEO about her problem. Because he has a team of people monitoring his correspondence, she got a result quicksmart - probably much quicker than if she'd started at the bottom!

Another good tip I've heard is to use the human resources site www.LinkedIn.com. Like Facebook for people's work lives, it allows you to search by company and find the names and job titles of all the people who work for an organisation. So if you're the resourceful type, you might be able to locate the *exact* person who can fix your problem, and drop them a little note to say hi.

But for goodness' sake, *be polite*. Be reasonable. Bear in mind it's just someone doing their job. People are much more likely to go into bat for you if you're not an arsehole.

And if that doesn't work . . .

STEP #2: Whinge in public

Once upon a time, cranky customers who couldn't get their complaints resolved used to stand outside the business's front office with a sandwich board strapped to their chest. Some still do!

But the internet has been a wonderful development

for both complainants and businesses – if not for the makers of sandwich boards. You can now rabble-rouse from the comfort of your own home and it can be just as effective.

The most common way to make a complaint public now is by posting it on social media.

Facebook and Twitter are the new 'shop window'. Most businesses resolve social media complaints as a priority because they don't like their dirty laundry hanging out in public. Big businesses have whole teams of people who just monitor comments and try to resolve them ASAP.

If Step #1 didn't resolve your issue, post a comment on the business's Facebook page and tag them in a tweet (if you're on Twitter).

Here's an example below from when my broadband service went down and I couldn't get a resolution on phone or live chat:

Joel Gibson
@joelgibson

Earth to @Optus - can't get through on phone, live chat or carrier pigeon to ask why my broadband service has been down for 24hrs, so trying Twitter. Is there anyone home?

5:31 PM - 10 Jan 2018

2 Retweets 1 Like

2 2 1

Once again, *be polite*. If you're rude on social media, there's nowhere to hide. Everyone can see you being a crank. (But a lame joke or two? That's perfectly ok.)

INSIDE INFO: Facebook has a very clever button for businesses that allows them to 'hide' your comment from all but you and your 'friends'. So the ruder you are, the less likely others are to end up seeing your complaint.

If none of the above works, it's time to …

STEP #3: Whinge to the regulator

When my wi-fi went down for a month, I tried both steps one and two above.

When I asked for compensation via my provider's live chat service, someone called Noah told me it was not their fault but the local electricity network's, and *he* lost his temper at *me*.

I also complained extensively on Twitter, but it was like whingeing in space, where no one can hear you scream.

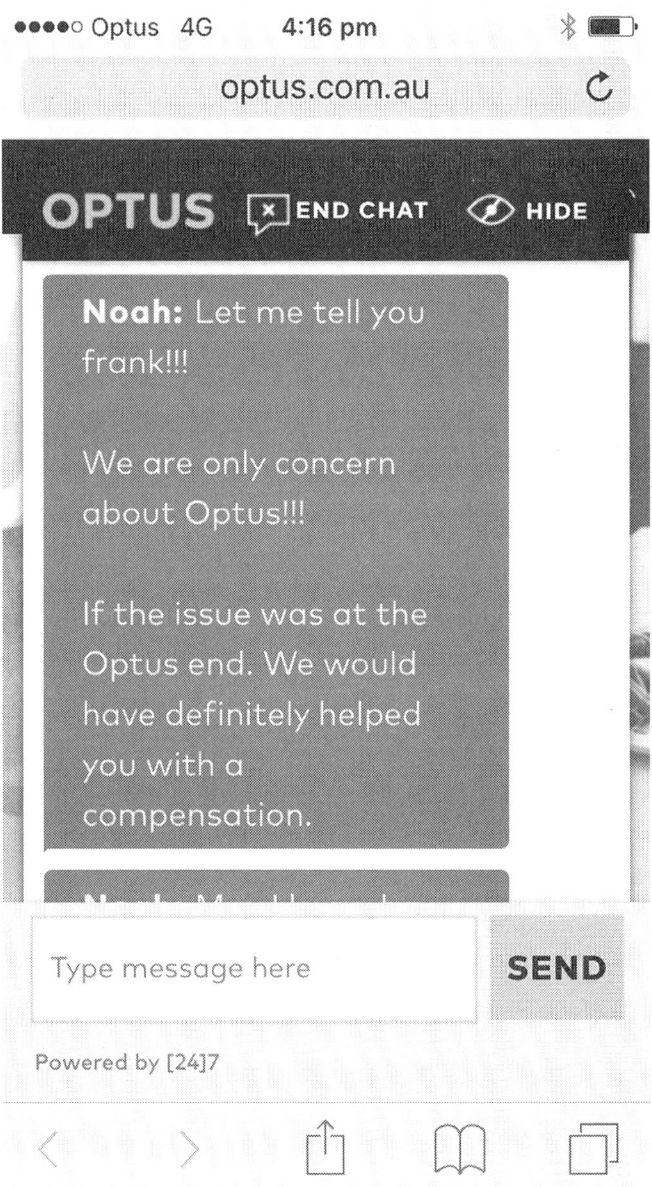
●●●●○ Optus 4G
4:16 pm
optus.com.au
OPTUS
END CHAT
HIDE
Noah: Let me tell you frank!!!
We are only concern about Optus!!!
If the issue was at the Optus end. We would have definitely helped you with a compensation.
Type message here
SEND
Powered by [24]7

But then my wife gave me a great tip - remember how being a good listener is one of the secrets to saving on your bills?

In Australia, if you make an official complaint to the national 'Telecommunications Industry Ombudsman' (TIO to his mates), your provider has to open a file for your complaint and allocate someone else internally to resolve it.

Many other industries operate similar processes for complaints.

So I complained to my new best mate 'TIO'. Here's what happened next:

- On 25 January I told the ombudsman I wanted the provider to: 'Restore service ASAP. Communicate with customers the progress of the fix regularly. Refund the month's broadband fees. Refund the month's mobile fees too (I am having to tether from my Optus mobile and using up all my data to cover the lack of wi-fi).'

- On 29 January, the ombudsman wrote to say they'd relayed the complaint to the provider.
- On 5 February, the wi-fi came back on and the provider called to say they would refund the month's wi-fi charges and the excess data charges on my mobile.
- And on 2 March, they contacted me to say they were crediting our account another $459.80 as compensation for the inconvenience!

You never know, but I think if I hadn't been a squeaky wheel and taken the complaint to the official channels, we wouldn't have got this result.

Unfortunately, sometimes it pays to be difficult. But it also pays to do it the smart way – after all, who wants to stand around all day with a sandwich board strapped to them?!

Here's the wording of my complaint to TIO, which you can use as a basis for your own complaint if you need to make one: the key is to keep a record of any communication with your provider so that you have *details* when the time comes to whinge, and to work out exactly what you can ask for as a solution.

(As we'll see in the 'Red Dog' trick in Chapter 9, you should ask for a lot. Ask for whatever you've missed out on, plus some form of compensation for the inconvenience. Don't hold back.)

TIO Complaint #2018/01/17251

Complaint description	No internet service to the area for 15 days so far. No proactive communication from Optus as to what the issue is or when it will be fixed. Only a reply to a tweet on Jan 17 stating 'Hey Joel :) Thanks for that. I can see from the note on the fault number that we're working with the power company to get this resolved as quickly as possible. Still no ETR – Marie'. Ausgrid has tweeted saying its work is not preventing Optus from fixing the issue.
Your preferred outcome	Restore service ASAP. Communicate with customers the progress of the fix regularly. Refund the month's broadband fees. Refund the month's mobile fees too (I am using up all my Optus mobile data to cover the lack of wi-fi).

CHAPTER 8
DAVID'S SLINGSHOT

When pint-sized David took on Goliath, he was battling the Old Testament equivalent of Arnie Schwarzenegger or The Rock.

But David had two things going for him.

One, he was blessed by God (a handy leg-up in life). And two, he was also blessed by technology, in the form of a humble slingshot.

We might not think of a slingshot as technology, but in 1020 BC it was probably the taser of its time.

The Old Testament story is a reminder that humans are unique among the animal kingdom in our ability to make tools to tackle complex challenges.

When we needed to fight bigger creatures - human or otherwise - we created weapons.

When we needed to get somewhere, we created the wheel and then the chariot, the train, the car and finally the plane (and then the, um, segway. . .).

And then we created possibly the most significant human invention of all time: the internet.

The internet is your equivalent of David's slingshot: it will help you win battles you never could have attempted before.

When you want to save on your bills and you're negotiating with a big, billion-dollar business with thousands of employees, you can feel a bit like David taking on Goliath.

The main reason is that it's not usually a level playing field. You're suffering from what economists call 'information asymmetry' – the business knows all about electricity or insurance or home loans and has thousands of customers they can study to understand the typical consumer.

Then there's little old you.

But the internet has changed the game. The internet has made it easier than ever before to find the right information to level that playing field (as long as you know where to look, and we'll tell you in Part 2 of this book).

Did you know, for example, that in most states there's a website that will tell you what the cheapest electricity deals are in your area and rank them in price order for you? You can check the market and switch your home over to the cheapest deal around in under ten minutes if you know how.

The traditional smoke and mirrors around home loans is now clearing too, thanks to a whole range of websites and tools that are putting it all out there for you to see.

A bit of smart internet research can save you hundreds or even thousands of dollars a year on your bills. And you can also switch online in minutes.

Don't have the internet at home? Not super confident with it? Go to the local library or ask someone for help, and read the tips in the second half of this book.

Because without the web, you're like David meeting Goliath without a rock or a slingshot.

True Story: Valeria from Queensland switches health funds and saves $872 a year. On her phone. At the gym!

So you think switching your health insurance policy is complicated? That it takes hours on the phone and isn't worth the hassle?

Oh ye of little faith! I give you Valeria from Queensland.

When we heard that a young mum in Queensland had saved $872 on her premium by switching to a new provider and plan, we were pretty chuffed.

But when we learnt that she'd done it entirely on her phone, while at the gym, we nearly fell out of our chairs!

'The switching process was very easy. I was actually at the gym and was able to fill out my form online on my phone, and it took, you know, just a few minutes,' Valeria said.

Valeria's a busy mum, personal trainer, health coach and wellness blogger @TheWellNest based on the Sunshine Coast.

After seeing one of our TV segments about the benefits of shopping around, she changed her health insurance to similar cover with a different fund and saved a whopping $872 a year on her base premium. She also got a $300 gift card as a bonus for joining the new fund.

'We were very close to dropping our cover because I was paying almost $400 a month, which is very, very expensive. So to cut that back was a huge saving for us and knowing that we have that peace of mind of cover is really important.'

So Valeria now has over $800 a year to spend on other things.

'It makes me feel like I can go for a little bit of a shop!' she laughed.

STOP PRESS: When I checked in with Valeria just before this book went to print, she told me she'd just switched again to another fund, and achieved even better value for her money. So lightning does strike twice.

CHAPTER 9
THE RED DOG

Like I said earlier, loyalty is all but dead in household bills. But it hasn't breathed its last gasp just yet. (Like Westley in *The Princess Bride*, it's just 'mostly dead'!)

I needed to include this final insider trick as an acknowledgment that there are indeed cases where it pays to be loyal.

I may be cynical but I'm not entirely one-eyed. And 'the Red Dog' is about showing loyalty to providers when (and *only* when) they show loyalty to you.

(I also needed to include this trick so I'd have an excuse to put a gratuitous picture of my dog in the book. This is Sunny. This is how he's been staring at me for pretty much the past six months while I wrote

Kill Bills!. He's not a red dog, but he's got some reddish patches. 'Mostly red', maybe!)

Dogs make us feel good about life, the universe and everything, because they're so darn loyal - for better or worse.

Some of us are like that as consumers: so very, very loyal, even when our providers don't do the right thing by us.

I'll explain below why that's completely natural - in fact, it's *more* human to be loyal than it is to be disloyal.

And there are a few rare examples where businesses do show loyalty to customers who deserve it, which also makes me feel good about the world.

Hence this final insider trick: 'the Red Dog'.

Red Dog is one of Australia's favourite movies. It's in the top ten highest-grossing Aussie films of all time.

Based on a true story and a book by Louis de Bernières, it's the story of a red kelpie without a master who attaches himself to John Grant, an American truck driver working in a WA iron ore mine.

When John has a motorbike accident and doesn't come home one day, Red Dog waits for him for weeks, and then goes out looking for him, covering much of Australia's vast Pilbara region between Perth and Darwin and even - according to one rumour - jumping a ship to Japan.

In the end, Red Dog dies lying next to John's grave and there's now a statue erected in his memory in Dampier, WA.

What does all that have to do with your latest bill?

Well, 'doing a Red Dog' is a calculated tactic whereby you go all-in with your loyalty to one provider, because the rewards are worth it.

I want to be clear that these cases are rare: usually, the *best* way to kill bills is to fight our own human nature, adopt the 'De Niro' attitude I've described earlier, embrace change and be ruthlessly disloyal.

But there are indeed times where a business will

reward you for your loyalty, and sometimes it makes perfect sense to give them loyalty in return.

So here are some examples:

Health insurance

Bonus limits: Some health funds will give you higher claim limits if you've been with them for longer. For example, your annual limit for dental might be $1000 in year one, but if you've been a member for five years, they'll increase it to $1200. Or you might be able to claim up to $50 per dental check-up, and that increases to $70 after a few years. Note that these bonus limits almost *always* apply to 'extras' treatments such as dental, orthodontic, physio and optometry - not to hospital treatments.

Verdict: *Nice-to-have, but for most of us they're not a reason to stay with a health fund if the base premium and the cover you're getting are not good value in themselves.*

Rewards programs: Some health funds now have rewards programs or link to other rewards programs so you can get rewards points, frequent flyer points, discounts on other bills or products.

Verdict: *Also nice-to-have, but not a good reason to stick with an over-priced policy.*

Home & car insurance

Multi-policy discounts: Providers who sell multiple products can sometimes reward you for taking more than one policy with them. You might get an extra 10 or 15% off your home insurance premium, for example, if you also have car insurance and/or landlord's insurance with Company X.

Verdict: *If you like the product and the price to begin with, this can be a real bonus. But don't take out a policy at a price that's not competitive and then rely on the multi-policy discount to make it better. Also, don't just assume they add up to more than the savings you'll get from shopping around. Often the starting price is high, so the multi-policy discount just brings your total back down to earth. (See the case study in Chapter 12.) Finally, businesses regularly change their policy on this one, I've found, so do check from time to time to see if you're still getting these savings.*

Rewards programs: Some insurance companies now have rewards programs or link to other rewards programs so you can get rewards points, frequent flyer points, discounts on other bills or products.

Verdict: *Also nice-to-have, but not an excuse to stick with an over-priced policy.*

Telcos

Bundling discounts: A bit like a multi-policy discount on insurance, telcos often give you a discount on the second or third product you take out with them. I get $20 a month off my mobile plan because I've got broadband with the same company, for example. The Telstra bundle with Foxtel is a classic example: Foxtel works out cheaper if you also take other telco products with Telstra.

Verdict: *Again, a good rule is: the price and product have to be competitive before the bundled discount, otherwise the bundle can become a trap that just locks you into more than one over-priced product. In Chapter 11, Telco, we'll see how you can get most of the elements in a Telstra bundle for about $600 a year less - if you're prepared to compromise.*

Rewards programs: Some telco companies now have rewards programs or link to other rewards programs so you can earn rewards points, frequent flyer points, discounts on other bills or products.

Verdict: *Also nice-to-have, but not a good reason to stick with an over-priced policy.*

Supermarkets

Petrol discounts: Shop at Coles or Woolies and you'll earn petrol discount vouchers, which you can cash in for 4c/l discount at participating fuel outlets.

Verdict: *Perhaps not surprisingly, Coles and Woolies' fuel outlets often sell petrol at about 4c/l more than the little independent outlets, so using these dockets can just make your petrol as cheap as the cheaper stations. But if that works for you, do it! The reality is, most of us choose a petrol station nearby so you need to hunt out the cheapest petrol in your area using a kit-bag of discount vouchers, petrol apps and inside info (more on this in Chapter 15).*

Rewards programs: Coles and Woolies also have very sophisticated rewards programs that are designed to keep you within their universe of stores and collect data about your habits that makes them better at selling to you. They reward you for using their supermarkets, their discount department stores, their bottle shops, their petrol stations, their credit cards, their insurance and their telco products.

Verdict: *At the most basic level, you have to spend $2000 at Coles or Woolies supermarkets to earn a $10 discount on your next shop, which ain't much of a reward. But these schemes are designed to multiply your rewards by up to six or seven times if you're prepared to use all of the services above. My view is you're better off being a Lone Ranger and looking for the best deal on each. But if you lived in a one-supermarket, one-servo, one-bottleshop town, for example, and they were all owned by the same company, you'd be mad not to go the full 'Red Dog'. It really depends on your personal circumstances.*

Why it's only human to want to be loyal

If you find it hard to act like Robert De Niro, you're only human. Most of us do!

Social scientists have proven that, as human beings, we prefer inertia to most forms of change - even when change is in our best interests.

This is because of two essential human traits that psychologists and economists have shown to be prevalent in experiment after experiment: they call them 'Status Quo Bias' and 'Loss Aversion'.

'Loss Aversion' is our curious tendency to feel losses more than we feel wins. The boffins estimate that losing something makes us twice as miserable as gaining something makes us happy.

A collection of Nobel Prize-winning economists have tested this with university students. They gave half of them a free mug and then asked them how much they'd be willing to give up the mug for. They also asked the students without mugs to say what they'd be willing to pay for a mug.

The students who had mugs wanted roughly twice the amount for their mugs than the other students were prepared to pay for them.

'Thousands of mugs have been used in dozens of replications of this experiment, but the results are nearly always the same,' writes one of the economists, Professor Richard Thaler, in his best-selling book *Nudge: Improving Decisions about Health, Wealth and Happiness*. 'Once I have a mug, I don't want to give it up. But if I don't have one, I don't feel an urgent need to buy one.'

In another experiment, half the class got mugs and half got chocolate bars worth the same amount. When asked if they wanted to switch, only one in ten students said yes.

Our Status Quo Bias is similar but not quite the same.

As human beings, we tend towards the status quo and avoid change unless it's really necessary. 'Better the Devil you know,' as the saying goes. There's example after example of this.

TV programmers know that if you win the 6pm news slot or the 7.30pm entertainment slot, you'll often go on to win the ratings for the rest of the evening. Because people prefer not to change the channel!

When streaming services give you a free trial, it's because they know that once they have your payment details, many of us won't cancel after a month, even if we're not using the service much.

Australians have about $670 billion in so-called 'MySuper' superannuation funds, which are the default fund regulated by government. Some of us may actively choose those funds, but most are probably just leaving them in the default fund because of Status Quo Bias.

Put Loss Aversion, Status Quo Bias and household bills together and what do you get?

Inertia! Blind loyalty! Laziness! Ripped off!

Those are just some of the words that get thrown around to explain why we don't switch and save more often.

Call it what you like - it's a very human response and if we want to pay as little as possible for our bills and save that money to spend on other things that make us and our families happy, we need to understand our own human nature and know when to fight against it.

Businesses know about Loss Aversion and Status Quo Bias and they use them to sell us stuff. Governments know about Loss Aversion and Status Quo Bias and they use them to try and protect us (from businesses, and also from ourselves).

We need to know about them too, if only because everybody else does! And when it comes to being a real Bill-Killer, a bit of self-knowledge goes a long way.

'Grandfathered' deals deserve the Red Dog treatment too

There's another example where it pays to be loyal: sometimes you're on a cracking deal they don't offer anymore and you'd be a mug to leave!

These so-called 'grandfathered' deals can be better than anything currently on the market because the market might have gone backwards since you locked them in, but the provider may be prepared to keep offering you the same product unless you decide to change.

So you have to apply some common sense: don't move for the sake of moving. Just be ready to.

True Story: I couldn't save my brother any money on his health insurance. Sorry, bro!

In case you think I'm suggesting you'll save hundreds of dollars every time you so much as glance at another product or provider, here's the sorry tale of my recent attempt to help my brother save a few bucks on his health insurance.

My bro is a regular switcher; he shops around and moves when he sees a good deal, so he doesn't usually need any help from me.

But he did ask me recently to take a look at some health insurance deals suggested to him by a comparison website, so I did.

What I found was that they couldn't beat the policy he was on for value. They were proposing a downgrade to save money, but it would have meant getting rid of some cover he wanted to keep.

He was on a plan that no longer exists (probably because it's far better than anything that's now available). The fund was probably losing money on him if he ever needed to claim, but they had decided to keep giving him that plan for as long as he wanted it.

Once we realised that, he decided it was best to stay put on this occasion.

So there you go - sometimes you *are* better off remaining loyal.

Congratulations, Grasshopper

You're now ready to kill some serious bill.

We've just run through nine insider tricks I've picked up over the years that you need to know if you want to pay bottom dollar for your bills.

In Part 1 we've also looked at some of the basic human traits we have to battle against to be an effective Bill-Killer. The path to eternal money-saving happiness is going to mean you need to keep the following in mind:

- Be a 'Price-Chaser' not a 'Sleeping Beauty'.
- Don't get paralysed by all the choice out there! Remember that 'good enough' is almost always good enough.
- Always have another offer to 'anchor' your negotiations with providers.
- Don't be afraid of change, or of losing things that aren't really that valuable anyway.
- Save your loyalty for those providers who show it to *you* first.

If you've read all of Part 1, you've now got all the

theory you need to kick some serious household bill backside.

In Part 2 we move on to the more practical stuff: the inside info you need to know about each bill, how to get a quick win, and then how to win over and over again throughout your lifetime - because no matter how good you are at keeping them under control, bills are like cane toads - they have a tendency to just keep on coming!

PART 2

9 MAJOR HOUSEHOLD BILLS (AND HOW TO KILL THEM)

HOW TO USE PART 2 OF THIS BOOK

In this second part of the book, I'll run through nine of the major household bills and give you the insider secrets that people who work in those industries know that you may not.

This is crucial if you want to keep on top of the cost of living, which never seems to stop rising.

Read this section from start to finish or just dip into the relevant chapter when you receive a big power bill, or your insurance renewal arrives with a massive premium increase, or you get that nagging feeling you're being shafted.

If you just need a quick win, there's a 'Quick Bill-Kill' at the start of each chapter to achieve a saving in the shortest possible time.

But if you *do* read it all, you'll pick up a 'Bill-Killer Belt' with each chapter you complete. Just like when the kids do karate, you'll start with White for energy, then move to Yellow for car & home insurance, Orange for health insurance, Green for Telco, Blue for credit cards, Purple for petrol, Brown for life insurance, Red for groceries and finally a Black belt for the big one: home loans.

By that stage you'll be a bona fide money-saving Ninja, ready to open your own dojo and teach others in the ways of #KillBills.

CHAPTER 10
ENERGY

Power bills have become one of the biggest 'barbecue-stoppers' in Australia, thanks to our electricity prices, which are some of the highest in the world.

In fact, according to one leading energy economist, South Australians had the world's highest electricity bills in 2017 (the same year they could have made the Olympic final for 'most blackouts').

This is not an event where you want to be the champ. But the good news about energy in Australia is that in some cases you can save over $2000 a year just by knowing how to find a cheap plan. And once you know how to do it, it's like riding a bike - you'll never pay top dollar again.

Australians pay highest power prices in world

Exclusive

Ben Potter and Andrew Tillett

Australian residential customers are paying the highest electricity prices in the world – two to three times more than American households – but experts say they need more than information to navigate the thicket of discounts and offers.

South Australian households are paying the highest prices in the world at 47.13¢ per kilowatt hour, more than Germany, Denm

Also, the biggest changes to energy offers in a generation kicked in on 1 July 2019, and these were designed to help solve Australia's energy affordability crisis.

In this section, I'll run you through the latest changes and tell you how to cash in.

Pressed for time? No worries. You can follow my 'Quick Bill-Kill' to get a win in under half an hour.

Or maybe you're ready to go the whole hog and learn all the inside info you need to know to kill power bills this year and next year and every year from here on in? Then read on . . .

At a glance

Potential saving	From $50 up to $2000 for an average household, depending on your state
Degree of difficulty	2 out of 5

Ideal time to save	Mid-July in most states, after retailers have announced their annual price changes. In Victoria, it's mid-January. But any time will work.
Time required to switch	Starting from 5–10 minutes to fill out the online form. Then up to 90 days waiting for your final meter read (during which time your old provider might try to win you back).
Top online tools	• OneBigSwitch.com.au, where I work! We aim to always have a Group-Discounted Offer available for our members. • energymadeeasy.gov.au is the government website and lists all advertised offers in NSW, South-east Qld and SA (in Victoria it's compare.energy.vic.gov.au and NSW has its own called energyswitch.service.nsw.gov.au) • Wattever.com.au is the most up-to-date commercial comparison site
If I could tell you one thing about energy bills it would be:	Switchers get the best deals (and they're often not advertised).

QUICK BILL-KILL: Energy

If you've got a substantial power bill, not a lot of time and you just need an easy win, here are four steps to a quick and dirty saving in under 20 minutes. (Note this only works in South-east Qld, NSW, Victoria and SA where switching is possible. Otherwise you'll have to flick through to 'other ways to save' below):

1. **Grab your last bill.** It should tell you how much electricity you used over the most recent quarter or month, the rates you're paying, and what discount you're getting.
2. **Go to the government website energymadeeasy.gov.au (or compare.energy.vic.gov.au in Victoria.** If you're in NSW and you have an email bill, go to energyswitch.service.nsw.gov.au). Enter your details. See which offers they recommend as the cheapest.
3. **Next, go to OneBigSwitch.com.au (where I work) and see what the current Group-Discounted Deal is in your state.** You've now got two super-cheap offers in your hot little hand. You're armed and dangerous. At this point, you have a choice: you can pick a winner and switch, or you can call your provider and ask if they can beat those deals. Here's that basic script again:

'Hi there, my name is [Robert De Niro/ Insert Your Name Here]. Can you please put me through to someone on your retention team? I've been a loyal customer of yours for _______ years and I'd like to stay on, but I've just received a really good offer from another provider and I think it might be a better deal than the one I'm on. _______ has offered me _______. I wondered whether you can match it or even beat it? If you can, I'll lock it in right now.'

4. **Once you decide whether to stay or switch, it will take about five minutes to fill out the form or complete the process over the phone.** You'll be amazed by how easy it is. (Got gas? You can repeat the process above or just take the gas offer that comes with your electricity offer if it looks up to scratch.)

Don't forget to tell us about your win! Post your saving to @OneBigSwitchAU and @KillBillsBook with the hashtag #KillBills and we'll share it with all the other Bill-Killers out there.

HARD TRUTH: 15% of us have been paying top dollar so that 85% of us don't have to

It's a long story and boring how we got ourselves into this situation, but the most important thing you need to know about power bills in Australia is this: about 15% of us have been paying some of the world's highest prices so that the rest could get bigger and bigger discounts.

Once you know that, you don't need to be Einstein to see that the key to saving on your power bills is this: be one of the 85%, not the 15%.

The good news is, the 85% is growing. More than 2 million Aussies now switch power companies each year, and reports by regulators say that you can save over $2000 by switching plans in some parts of the country.

Another piece of good news is that the government is finally doing something about this shemozzle, which has punished the people who are not capable of shopping around for themselves: people like the elderly, those who don't know how to use a computer or don't have easy access to one, and those who just don't have the confidence or the time to stick up for themselves.

Since 1 July 2019, people who do nothing to shop around for a cheaper electricity plan will be put onto a new 'default offer' or 'reference price' in the eastern states that's about $150–$250 *cheaper* on average than the old 'standing offers' they were placed on previously.

But here's the thing: you still need to shop around to maximise your savings. 80–90% of the deals out there are still cheaper than these new 'default offers', and the best offers available to 'Price-Chasers' are hundreds of dollars cheaper.

The good news is: it's never been easier to find the cheapest deal, because all discount offers now have to be compared to that new 'default offer', so you can finally make apples-for-apples comparisons, which wasn't possible before.

So if you want to kill this bill, you *must* actively switch - or at least upgrade with the same provider - every year or two. The market is constantly moving and there are three rules to remember about the Australian energy market:

1. Switchers get the best deals.
2. Switchers get the best deals.
3. And switchers get the best deals!

The best insider tricks to use on . . . energy bills

The De Niro

As I explained in Part 1, this trick is more an 'attitude' than an 'act'. Like Robert De Niro's bank-robber character in the movie *Heat*, you gotta at least be *prepared* to walk away if you want access to the best energy deals.

In the energy market, loyalty has gone the way of the dodo – it's as dead as most of the characters by the end of *Heat*.

There are some examples of loyalty schemes in insurance and groceries and other household bills, and a few of them are worthwhile participating in.

But I can't think of a single meaningful reward I've seen for staying with your provider of electricity and gas, and I've been looking at power bills every day for the past eight years.

In fact, it's generally the opposite – perversely, the best deals are offered *only* to new customers or to customers who have one foot out the door, De Niro-style.

Don't believe me? Then take the word of the regulator, the Australian Energy Market Commission, who says this:

> “*Consumers tend to only get a better deal if they leave or threaten to leave a retailer.*”

Many retailers will also put you on their worst 'zero discount' plan if you move house or your discount expires – it's up to you to ask for a better one.

INSIDE INFO: Movers often pay top dollar. You can't take your fantastic energy deal with you when you move. You need to re-contract on a new deal, or they'll put you on a dud deal, which can cost you thousands more over time.

This happened to us last time we moved house. Luckily I realised pretty quickly. I then called up and went from no discount to 28% off in a single phone call, because I let them know I was prepared to walk for a better deal.

True Story: Peter from SA moves house, then saves $2000 by switching

About 2 million Aussies change electricity plans each year, and almost half of them are moving house!

But a lot of movers just want to make sure the lights come on and don't have the time or energy to ensure their deal is a good one.

Power companies know this, so they sometimes

sell their most expensive offers to movers – often through real estate agents, mortgage brokers and other people who have access to movers.

So it was for Peter from the Barossa Valley in South Australia (that's him above), who moved house and agreed to let his real estate agent organise an energy deal for him. Bad idea.

'The first two bills were outrageous, totalling just under $4000 for six months!' he told us. 'When I complained to them, they didn't want to know even though I threatened to change. So I moved.'

The agent had put him on a zero-discount 'standing offer', probably pocketing a commission for doing so, and Peter ended up paying top dollar every time he switched on the telly or the lights.

Over the next six months, thanks to a large new pay-on-time discount, Peter's bills added up to less than half of that initial amount. He saved over $2000.

'This is such a huge difference,' he told me. 'I'm so happy I changed.'

Coming soon to Australian power bills: automated switching services

If you just wish someone else would do it all for you, you may not have to wait very long.

In recent times, one of the most interesting developments in household power bills around the world has been the appearance of a number of services experimenting with 'automated energy switching'.

When you sign up to these services, they take over your energy account for you and switch you to a new plan - it could be annually, or whenever they find you something cheaper.

Sometimes they charge a fee, sometimes they don't.

CHOICE experimented with this in Australia but then paused their $100-a-year trial. One Big Switch (where I work) is investigating it as I write this book. There are maybe a dozen examples already operating in the UK and the US, so it's only a matter of time.

Aussie regulators are open to the idea. In its landmark report into power prices in 2018, the ACCC said it was looking into 'whether changes ... are required to encourage [third party] switching providers to start up in Australia'.

Another development will also make these services more likely: the Consumer Data Right was due to begin in late 2019, and it says you have a right to access your energy data and show it to whomever you like.

Now, most people would rather a poke in the eye

with a blunt stick than to have to read their energy usage data, but energy retailers and automated switching services are not most people.

If they can get access to your data (with your permission), they could potentially save you thousands by always moving you to an ideal plan for your home, whenever the market changes.

So watch this space . . .

The Under-the-Table Deal

Most power companies have offers they never show to the general public. These can be significantly better than their best publicly advertised discount.

If you want the cheapest electricity going, it's often going to be on one of these 'under-the-table' deals.

They might offer these deals to a special partner that has a large audience (like One Big Switch; or a footy club; or a motoring club), or they might offer them to their staff, or they might offer them as 'retention deals' to someone who is leaving. But they don't usually broadcast them to the world. You have to ask.

The key to getting access to these deals is leverage – and you can get that by being a member of one of the groups I've listed above: you need to join a big buying group, or get on the payroll, or threaten to leave for another provider!

INSIDE INFO: I've seen employees of power companies get discounts that are 12% *more* than their best advertised offer, but unfortunately this is the hardest group to join out of the three examples I gave above – there's no way to get that sort of deal without actually working there ... On the other hand, joining a buying group or 'doing a De Niro' is simple.

If you get access to one of these deals and your current provider tries to match it or beat it, you can end up in a 'Dutch auction' between two providers, and that's when you know you've already won.

In that situation, you're almost certain to walk away with an absolute killer deal, whichever retailer you choose.

True Story: Melinda saves $588 a year by switching to an Under-the-Table Deal

In my day job over the past eight years, I've seen hundreds of people save big bucks using Under-the-Table energy deals.

From time to time we go out and meet them, and those are my favourite days in (or out of) the office because it reminds us why we go to work each day.

One of the loveliest families I've met was Melinda and her two daughters Grace and Indii-Annah in Sydney's south-west.

The family needs to use a lot of power to maintain a certain temperature range in their home because of Indii's disability so there wasn't much more they could do to reduce their usage.

But there were much bigger discounts available than they were getting and, based on analysis of their old bills, we estimate they saved $588 a year by switching to a group-discounted deal we had negotiated.

'We switched from Dodo to a 30% discount with Alinta . . . and you could easily see the savings straight away,' Melinda said. 'It was super easy . . . it took about five minutes and I was done. The savings, as you can see, are ridiculous.'

The Squeaky Wheel

Been overcharged by your energy retailer? Unfairly disconnected? Bullied by a pushy salesperson?

More than 100,000 households around the country report a problem with their retailer each year. That's 2000 a week, or almost 300 of us every day!

So if you need to complain about a power company, you'll have plenty of company, and there are some well-organised systems in place to help you.

INSIDE INFO:

Psssst: If the complaint relates to a problem with your meter, an outage or other supply issue, you actually need to contact your energy distributor – that's the company that owns the poles and wires that bring the power to your home.

How do I know who my bloody distributor is, I hear you ask? Good question! You can check your bill, ask your retailer (who sends you the bill), or look for more info here: www.aer.gov.au/consumers/making-a-complaint/who-is-my-distributor

For complaints to do with your *retailer*, the best approach is to follow the 'Squeaky Wheel' strategy I explained in Part 1:

STEP #1:

Contact the retailer. Tell them (*politely but firmly!*) what the problem is and what you want them to do to fix it. If they don't agree, ask to speak to a manager and tell them the same thing.

Write down their name, the time of the call or email, and their response. Ask for their email address so you can put your complaint and your request in writing to them, to ensure they have a record of it. Write down a reference number too, if they provide one.

If you still don't get a resolution . . .

STEP #2:

Take it public. Post a (*polite but firm, remember!*) comment on their Twitter and Facebook pages. Wait 24 hours.

If you *still* don't get a resolution . . .

STEP #3:

Make it official. Contact the energy ombudsman in your state or territory and dob on them!

It's a free service and they'll try to resolve your issue. Best of all, they'll make your retailer take you seriously: NSW Energy & Water Ombudsman:

www.ewon.com.au/

Energy & Water Ombudsman Victoria:
www.ewov.com.au/
Energy & water Ombudsman Queensland:
www.ewoq.com.au/
Energy & Water Ombudsman SA:
ewosa.com.au/
Energy & Water Ombudsman WA:
www.ombudsman.wa.gov.au/energyandwater/
Energy Ombudsman Tasmania:
www.energyombudsman.tas.gov.au/
Energy Ombudsman ACT: www.acat.act.gov.au/

The Moving Target

This trick relates to bills where the product is changing so fast that you need to regularly upgrade or you'll get left behind.

Energy bills are a moving target because the discounts often expire after a year, and also because the energy market is so volatile.

Every month, the energy market changes and just about every month, a different provider comes out cheapest.

I'm often asked which provider is the best or the cheapest, but the answer to that question changes all the time. They're all selling the same electrons so you need to look at the offer, even more so than the provider.

Businesses go through cycles: sometimes their goal is to acquire *new* customers and they drop their prices, sometimes their goal is to retain current customers and increase the profits they're making from them, so they raise their prices.

Take your eye off the moving target and your good plan can become a poor one.

The key here is that discounts are constantly changing and tariffs change (usually upwards, of course) *at least once a year*. So you need to check your plan is still a corker *at least once a year*. It's a no-brainer.

If this sounds like a lot of work, it doesn't have to be. At the top of this chapter there's a 20-minute 'Quick Bill-Kill' you can do once a year and you'll be laughing all the way to the bank.

KILLER STAT: For an average-sized household, there's usually only about $100–$200 a year between the top five to ten deals at any given time.

Don't sweat it too much if your energy deal isn't #1 cheapest.

Remember the wise words of Barry Schwartz from Part 1 of this book:

"'Good enough' is almost always good enough."

The Elizabeth Taylor

The energy industry has been one of the greatest exponents of the 'Honeymoon Strategy' pricing model: they often win you over with a very cheap one-year deal and then raise the price and hope to make money out of you in later years if you don't leave.

This happens because of two factors: annual price rises, and discounts that expire. In most states, tariffs usually go up each July (or January in Victoria). Meanwhile, after your 12-month discount ends, you usually get bumped to a low discount, or no discount at all.

I can't say I've ever tested this one, but it's said that if you put a frog in a pot of boiling water it will leap out. But put it in a pot of cold water and slowly heat it up, and you'll end up with a cooked frog (and probably a charge for animal cruelty. Do *not* try this at home. It's a metaphor.)

The point of the boiling frog metaphor is that when things change gradually around us, sometimes we don't notice until it's too late.

And so it is with our power bills. Even a very good electricity deal can turn into an unhappy marriage over the course of a year, once the rates change and the discount expires.

So you need to be like Elizabeth Taylor and switch providers or plans regularly, enjoying the benefits of honeymoon after honeymoon!

It's also one of the easiest products to switch: you can fill out a form in about five minutes, there's no interruption to your supply and everyone's selling basically the same product.

True Story: My dad does a Liz Taylor and saves $1500 on his power bill

After 40 years of feeling like I didn't listen enough to his pearls of wisdom, my dad finally got his revenge.

On TV and in the newspapers, I'd been banging on for a few years now about shopping around and switching energy providers to maximise your discount.

I assumed he'd been listening, but when I asked him to send me his bill, lo and behold he was on a gargantuan, world-beating, jaw-dropping discount of . . . zero!

Dad lives down the coast from Sydney, on a big block in the bush with no gas, and his electricity bill was a whopper - about $1700 a quarter.

But like about 1 in 7 Australians, he hadn't recently shopped around or asked his provider for a better discount. He didn't think he was able to switch in the area where he lived. So he was paying top dollar.

This is not unusual - after all, until the last 20 years or so switching was not possible. Most of us had only one option - the local government-owned supplier (which is still the case for West Australians, the NT, Tasmanians and North Queenslanders).

Switching only started when power companies were privatised and pricing was deregulated to make them compete against one another. About a million Australians have still never switched.

So I upgraded my dad to a 28% discount for 12 months with the same provider (he didn't even have to switch in this case), and he saved an estimated $1500 over the next year.

And we agreed to listen to each other more.

David's Slingshot

Thanks to the internet, it's never been easier to find a cheap power deal and there's never been more help available.

There's now a government website called Energy Made Easy (energymadeeasy.gov.au) that lists every plan that's generally available (in Victoria it's called Victorian Energy Compare (compare.energy.vic.gov.au) and NSW also has another one that scans your email bill automatically (energyswitch.service.nsw.gov.au).

These sites even include some - but not all - of the 'under-the-table deals' that are available to members of certain organisations like One Big Switch or the motoring clubs NRMA, RACV, RACQ, RACWA & RAA.

All you do is grab your latest bill, punch the numbers in and it will show you most of the cheapest offers around right now, in rank order. It's a piece of cake.

Don't want to do it yourself? That's easy too. There are any number of commercial sites that will compare deals or source special offers for you, including:

- **OneBigSwitch.com.au** - declaration: this where I work. But I reckon we do a bloody good job. We have a single group-discounted offer at a time that's not available to the general public and that you can compare to what you're on, or we can get someone to compare it for you.
- **Wattever.com.au** - the most comprehensive non-government comparison website that updates offers as they change. But it does not have a call centre.
- **ISelect.com.au** - the most-used non-government comparison website. Requires a phone number, so it's probably more for those who want help comparing multiple deals over the phone.
- **ElectricityWizard.com.au** - similar to iSelect, this site requires a phone number, so it's for those who want help comparing over the phone.
- **9Saver.com.au** - a sister-site to One Big Switch, and similar. But the special offer is often a different one.
- **FiftyUpClub.com.au** - another sister-site to One Big Switch, designed for consumers aged 50-plus, where the special offer is often different.

32 Other Ways to Save on Energy around the Home

If you've done all you can to ensure your plan is cheap, or if you're in a state where you can't switch, the only other option for saving on power bills is to *use less*!

Here are 32 hacks to help you do that – do them all and it could add up to over $1000 in a year.

1. **Ditch the beer fridge.** They tend to be older appliances and therefore less energy efficient, and can chew through more than $250 a year.
2. **What's that? It'd be un-Australian to ditch it?** Alright, alright. Then just turn the beer fridge off in between times and turn it back on a few hours before your big event.
3. **Dial the heater down.** Men are most comfortable at about 22 degrees and women at about 24 degrees. So don't start at 25 degrees in winter as it may be unnecessary, especially if the house is full of blokes! Start low, see if it's comfortable, and only go hotter if you need to – every extra degree of temperature can add about $100 over the year.
4. **Dial the air con up!** Same principle. When cooling your home down, start with a higher target temperature such as 24 degrees first and see if it's comfortable before blasting out the icy-cold air.
5. **Avoid bar heaters and fan heaters** if you can. Reverse cycle air conditioners, for example, are two to 2.5 times more efficient. Gas is even better.
6. **Insulate.** Choose window coverings, door snakes and double-glazing. Insulation of any kind is hugely helpful in keeping a consistent temperature.
7. **Avoid 'vampire power'.** This is the power that unused appliances can 'suck' from your

power points. You can save about 10% by turning appliances off at the power point when not using them.

8. **Stars matter.** A three-star fridge/freezer can be $900 cheaper than a one-star appliance over the life of the machine. This is also a good reason to consider upgrading appliances sometimes, even if there's an initial cost to buy a new one.
9. **Don't overheat your hot water.** Try 50–60 degrees. Every degree there saves about 1% of your water heating cost. It's also safer, especially if there are small kids around who might turn a hot tap on without realising.
10. **Get gas.** Natural gas can prove to be a cheaper way to heat your home or your hot water and is well worth investigating - but there will be a change-over cost. A new gas hot water service or a good new gas heater can cost around $1000.
11. **Use timers** to control heating and cooling. Don't be slack: turn off appliances if you don't need them.
12. **Only heat or cool the rooms you are using**, rather than the whole house. Close the doors and insulate the room you're using. Cuddle each other!
13. **Put a jumper on**, as my mother used to say! Dress for the season and you won't need as much heating or cooling in the first place.
14. **Keep your oven serviced.** Keep the seals tight and oven clean to ensure no heat is wasted.

15. **Clean the filters** on the rangehood regularly. Vent the exhaust to outside your home and use the exhaust fan on the lowest speed.
16. **Stack the dishwasher** and don't run it until it's completely full. Same with the washing machine. Use cold water where possible.
17. **Electric fan-type ovens** are more efficient than conventional ovens.
18. **Gas hot water** uses less power than electrical hot water services. But solar hot water uses even less than gas.
19. **Shift your usage.** If you're on a plan that has off-peak or 'controlled load' rates, you can save about $260 a year by using washing machines, dishwashers or heating during off-peak times. Turn them on when you go to bed.
20. **Speaking of 'un-Australian'**, fill in or cover over your backyard swimming pool if you never use it. A pool pump can cost anywhere from $600 to $1500 a year to run and a spa costs about $240.
21. **No way?** Then run the pool or spa at night on an off-peak tariff or controlled load meter to minimise the cost.
22. **Clean pool filters often** to maximise your pump's efficiency.
23. **Cover it up.** An insulated cover on pools and spas will save money.

24. **Again, solar or gas** is cheaper than electricity for heating pools.
25. **Take shorter showers.** Did you know showering can make up to 60 per cent of your hot water usage?
26. **A shower uses less energy** than a bath - especially if you shower in twos!
27. **Spin dry** before hanging out a load of washing, rather than using the dryer for the whole job.
28. **Clean the dryer's lint filter** regularly. Or ditch the dryer altogether if you live in a dry part of the country. It may take a little longer but it sure saves a lot of money.
29. **Install solar panels.** The big government concessions are over, but panels can still cut your costs, especially if you use a lot of your energy during daylight hours.
30. **Use your appliances during the day** if you have solar power, so that they run for free.
31. **Switch off lights** in those rooms that aren't being used. It may seem a very obvious move but as any parent will attest, it's a constant battle!
32. **Opt for energy-efficient lightbulbs** - try CFL (compact fluorescent lamp) or the longer-lasting LED globes - over incandescent globes. Some of these bulbs are also dimmable.

TIGHTARSE TIP: Some states such as NSW and Victoria will subsidise the 'retro-fit' installation of LED light globes so that it costs you almost nothing. Just google 'LED energy efficiency retrofit' in your state to see if there's a current scheme.

Everything you wanted to know about power bills (and then some . . .)

Why are Australia's power bills so high?

We could be here all day answering this. But here's the short version: Australia has some of the world's highest power prices because they doubled in about a decade from 2007 to 2017 (see the graph below). The main reason was poor policy: a series of government stuff-ups meant that first the cost of transporting power skyrocketed, and then the cost of generating power skyrocketed. And all of it was passed on to you and me – the lucky end-user.

How did energy offers change on 1 July 2019?

In 2019 we saw the biggest changes to energy offers in South-east Qld, NSW, Victoria and SA since power bills

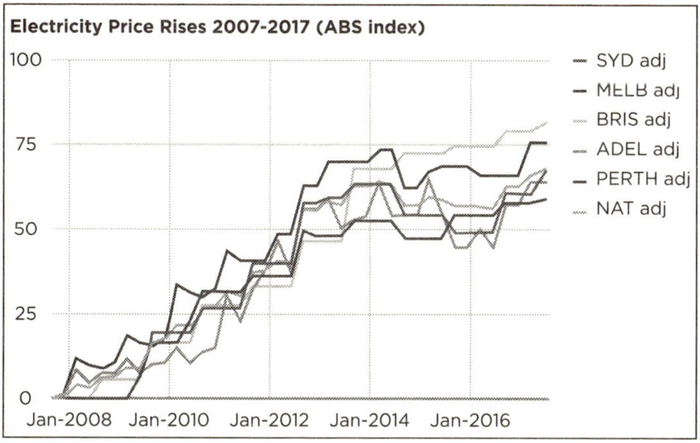

were privatised and deregulated in the 1990s and the noughties.

These changes didn't alter what you have to do to find a cheap plan (you still need to shop around and switch from time to time).They also didn't do much to change the actual price of our power.

They just (hopefully) made it easier to find a cheap plan.

There are two key things that changed on 1 July 2019:

1. People who do *nothing* and don't shop around are better off because they'll pay the new benchmark 'default offer' or 'reference price', which is cheaper than the old 'standing offers' by:
   - between $129 and $181 for New South Wales (depending on distribution zone)
   - $118 for South-east Queensland

- $171 for South Australia
- between $310 and $450 for Victoria (depending on distribution zone)

2. People who *do* shop around can pay hundreds of dollars less still, and best of all, we can now compare the cheapest offers more easily because *all* discounted deals must now be compared to that new 'default offer' or 'reference price' above.

To give you an example, below are two hypothetical energy deals. I've shown how they would have been described *before* the 2019 changes, and how they're now described *after* the changes.

Before 2019, retailers could apply their discounts to different rates. This created a crazy situation where a no-discount offer was sometimes cheaper than a 30% discount offer. You needed a calculator or a PhD in maths to work out what was cheapest!

As the table below shows, Deal #2 used to look better even though it was more expensive.

After 2019, we have apples-for-apples comparisons. Those offers now have to be compared to the *same* benchmark bill, so you can see that Deal #1 is really the cheapest offer:

	DEAL #1	DEAL #2
BEFORE 2019		
Advertised Discount	0%	30%
Discount applies to:	Low Rates	High Rates
Annual Bill	$1700	$1800
AFTER 2019		
Advertised Discount	15%	10%
Discount applies to:	Default Offer/ Reference Price	Default Offer/ Reference Price
Annual Bill	$1700	$1800

TIGHTARSE TIP: If you're in Victoria, your state government went even further than other states in July 2019. Your retailer will now have to tell you how much cheaper their 'best offer' is on all your bills, so keep an eye out for that notice in the top left corner. See the example below.

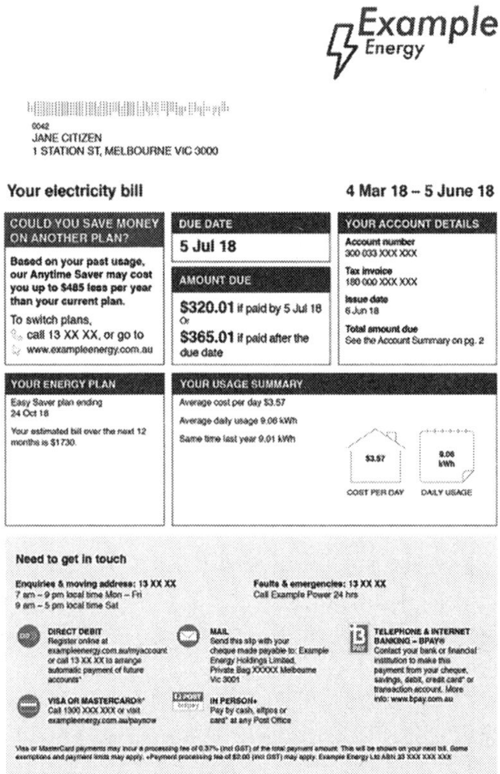

Example Energy

0042
JANE CITIZEN
1 STATION ST, MELBOURNE VIC 3000

Your electricity bill **4 Mar 18 – 5 June 18**

COULD YOU SAVE MONEY ON ANOTHER PLAN?
Based on your past usage, our Anytime Saver may cost you up to $485 less per year than your current plan.
To switch plans, call 13 XX XX, or go to www.exampleenergy.com.au

DUE DATE
5 Jul 18

AMOUNT DUE
$320.01 if paid by 5 Jul 18
Or
$365.01 if paid after the due date

YOUR ACCOUNT DETAILS
Account number
300 033 XXX XXX
Tax invoice
180 000 XXX XXX
Issue date
6 Jun 18
Total amount due
See the Account Summary on pg. 2

YOUR ENERGY PLAN
Easy Saver plan ending 24 Oct 18
Your estimated bill over the next 12 months is $1730.

YOUR USAGE SUMMARY
Average cost per day $3.57
Average daily usage 9.06 kWh
Same time last year 9.01 kWh
$3.57 COST PER DAY
9.06 kWh DAILY USAGE

Need to get in touch

Enquiries & moving address: 13 XX XX
7 am – 9 pm local time Mon – Fri
9 am – 5 pm local time Sat

Faults & emergencies: 13 XX XX
Call Example Power 24 hrs

DIRECT DEBIT
Register online at exampleenergy.com.au/myaccount or call 13 XX XX to arrange automatic payment of future accounts*

VISA OR MASTERCARD*
Call 1300 XXX XXX or visit exampleenergy.com.au/paynow

MAIL
Send this slip with your cheque made payable to: Example Energy Holdings Limited, Private Bag XXXXX Melbourne Vic 3001

IN PERSON+
Pay by cash, eftpos or card* at any Post Office

TELEPHONE & INTERNET BANKING – BPAY®
Contact your bank or financial institution to make this payment from your cheque, savings, debit, credit card* or transaction account. More info: www.bpay.com.au

Visa or MasterCard payments may incur a processing fee of 0.37% (incl GST) of the total payment amount. This will be shown on your next bill. Some exemptions and payment limits may apply. +Payment processing fee of $2.00 (incl GST) may apply. Example Energy Ltd ABN 33 XXX XXX XXX

Should I get solar?

It's estimated that solar panels will save an average household about $500 a year on average, so do the maths. On those numbers, if you've got a good roof for it, and you're likely to be in the house for a while, you can spend $5000 and you'll make it back in about ten years. Even if you move out, it might add to the value of your home when you sell it.

What about batteries?

It's the future, for sure. But right now they'll cost you $10,000 or more and we don't know yet how many charges the first generation of batteries will last for. So by all means go for it if you're an early adopter, or you just love the idea of being energy-independent. But I'll be waiting until the price comes down a bit - which it will. It's also possible that governments will subsidise the take-up of batteries the way they did with solar panels - and those who took up the government assistance to get panels laughed all the way to the bank.

Who can switch?

Anyone in NSW, Victoria, South Australia or South-east Queensland (the 'Energex Zone') can switch electricity and gas retailers. In WA, only gas is switchable. In Tasmania, North Queensland, and the NT you still have no choice, unfortunately - all you can do for now is look for ways to use less power.

How does a switch work?

Your retailer 'owns your meter', as the lingo in the industry goes. When you switch, a new retailer takes over that 'ownership'. If you have a smart meter (like most Victorians do), that changeover will happen after the ten-day cooling-off period. If it's not a smart meter (like most people in the rest of Australia), you'll have to wait for your next scheduled meter read (which is usually once every quarter, although sometimes your new retailer will request a 'special meter read' to get you switched over more quickly. Ask them).

Is switching worth it?

I've seen some people save over $1000 in a matter of minutes, so yes. Damn right it's worth it! But obviously, if you're already on a good deal, the potential saving will be smaller. Also, many people end up getting a much better offer to stay from their current provider once they've got a foot out the door. These are called 'retention' or 'win-back' offers. So, at the risk of sounding like a broken record . . . you need to *at least be prepared* to switch to get the best deals.

What can go wrong?

Not much. Your supply won't be disconnected when you switch providers – it's just the biller that changes. About the worst thing that can happen is that two retailers end up in a fight over who 'owns' your account. If this happens, you need to make it clear to them both who you want your provider to be, and if that doesn't work, be a 'squeaky wheel' and contact the ombudsman (see above).

What if I've got solar?

For you there is one extra factor to consider, on top of discounts and underlying rates – and that's the Solar Feed-in Tariff you can receive for selling your solar energy back into the power grid. There are two types of Feed-in Tariffs (FiTs): government and retailer FiTs. Those who got in early enough might still be receiving large government FiTs, which were offered for a limited time to encourage take-up of solar. But most solar households now just get retailer FiTs, which range from about 6c to 22c per kWh depending on your retailer and your state. As usual, shop around for a big FiT if you sell a lot of energy back in to the grid. If you use most of your solar energy, a good discount might be more important to you than the FiT.

What's the best deal for solar customers?

This all depends what sort of household you are. Are you home when the sun is up, using all your solar power? If so, you'll probably just want a nice big fat discount on any electricity you have to buy from the grid after dark. Are you out during the day and not using your solar power? If so, you might want to maximise your FiT so you can sell the power you generate back into the electricity grid for top dollar. There's no simple answer when it comes to solar - sorry!

What if I can't pay my bill?

Every retailer must have a 'hardship program' for people in your situation. Ask them about it. It will make it possible for you to negotiate a payment plan with the retailer. They're not supposed to just cut you off, but you need to ask to be put on this program to avoid disconnection, so do speak up!

Am I eligible for any government freebies?

Quite possibly. All states have rebates and concessions, and they vary depending on where you are. If you've got a concession card or you're on a low income, it's worth checking whether you qualify for some assistance. These change regularly but here is a list of state government websites to check:

NSW:

www.resourcesandenergy.nsw.gov.au/energy-consumers/financial-assistance/rebates

Vic:

services.dhhs.vic.gov.au/annual-electricity-concession

Qld:

www.qld.gov.au/community/cost-of-living-support/electricity-gas-rebates

www.dnrme.qld.gov.au/energy/initiatives/affordable-energy-plan

SA:

www.sa.gov.au/topics/care-and-support/financial-support/concessions/energy-bill-concessions

www.sa.gov.au/topics/care-and-support/financial-support/concessions/cost-of-living-concessions

WA:
www.wa.gov.au/service/community-services/financial-assistance/apply-energy-concession

Tas:
www.concessions.tas.gov.au/concessions/electricity_and_heating

ACT:
www.assistance.act.gov.au/adult/utilities/energy_concession

What if I'm moving house?

Then you *must* pick a new plan. You can't take your old one with you. That's why movers make up almost half of the people who switch each year. Make sure you choose a good plan when moving because if you let someone else choose it for you, you'll often end up on a dud, zero-discount deal.

Who has the best electricity?

This is one shop where everyone is selling more or less the same thing; the only differences are how they price it, how they deal with their customers, and maybe where they source it. A well-known brand does *not* have more reliable electricity than an unknown brand: they might have a better smartphone app or more people in their call centre, but the electrons they sell are the same.

Also, when you hear that certain power companies are 'cheap' or 'expensive', it's often a myth. While some have consistently high or low prices, most go back and forth between being near the top of the ladder or near the bottom, based on which cycle their business is going through (see 'The Moving Target' above). There's usually about $100–$200 a year between the top ten offers on the market, so don't shop around based on brands: shop around based on price.

True Story: I've been around a bit!

I confess: I am a total tart when it comes to my power providers.

Over the years, I've been in relationships with EnergyAustralia, AGL, Origin Energy, Click Energy, Powershop, and Alinta Energy.

That's because a good deal sometimes turns into a not-as-good deal after a year or more, and I switch when I see a better offer come along.

As a result, I often get myself into a Dutch auction between two providers who are both trying to win me over. I've probably switched providers half a dozen times in the past decade.

I estimate that it's saved me thousands of dollars over that time.

What about GreenPower?

Accredited GreenPower costs a bit more but most retailers will now give you the option of saying you want, say 25%, 50% or 100% of your power to be green. This doesn't mean the energy you use is actually from solar or wind or hydro - once the power goes into the grid it's all mixed together into a big electricity soup - but it does mean your retailer will ensure they buy the equivalent amount of power from green sources.

INSIDE INFO: Not all environmentally friendly electricity is accredited as 'GreenPower', because of a quirk in the legislation.

To qualify as 'accredited' GreenPower, it must have come from a renewable energy generator that was added to the national energy network after 1997, which rules out some sources such as hydro-electricity which already existed at the time. It's a bit unfair at times. For example, the company Momentum Energy gets its electricity from Tasmanian Hydro, but it's not allowed to call that energy 'GreenPower'. It does, however, like a lot of others, offer GreenPower to those who request it.

Who's the greenest power company?

Greenpeace looks at this each year and produces a 'Green Electricity Guide' ranking the various retailers according to 'the emissions intensity of the power stations they own, their investments in and policy positions on renewable energy and fossil fuels, their deals for solar consumers, their carbon offset products, their promotion of energy efficiency and demand management, and their corporate transparency and sustainability reporting'. Powershop (whose energy is not all green but is 100% carbon offset) comes out on top with five stars most years, while Diamond Energy and Energy Locals are others that rank near the top. Out of the Big Three, AGL and Origin got 3.5 stars in 2019 and EnergyAustralia got 3 stars.

Congratulations, Grasshopper. You've earned your first Bill-Killing Belt

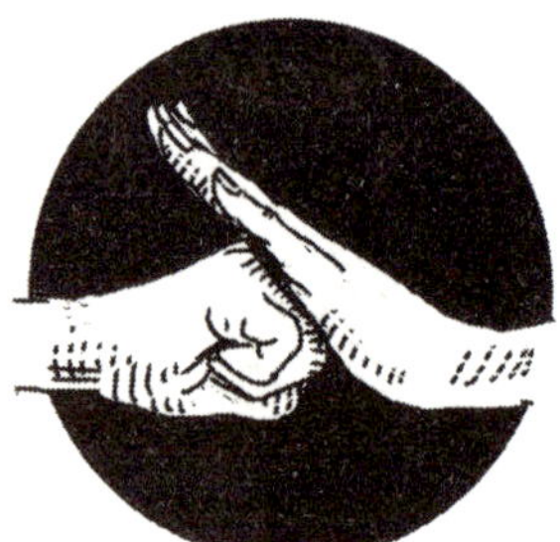

If you've read this chapter from start to finish, it's time to collect your first Bill-Killing Belt. Just like when kids learn karate, the first belt is a plain but stylish White one.

Energy is always first or second when Australians are asked which bills worry them the most, so hopefully by now you've got what you need to kill off that anxiety and save hundreds of dollars.

Nice work, Grasshopper. Next up: it's telco time.

CHAPTER 11
TELCO

Like energy, we've all got a telco bill. There's no avoiding it. Home broadband is fast becoming a necessity rather than a luxury, and . . .

KILLER STAT: There are more mobile phones than people in Australia!

The good news for anyone who wants to kill this bill is, it's probably the easiest one of the lot to compare online, thanks to the new super-powers bestowed on us by the internet.

The tough bit with a telco is deciding what data limits and speeds and features you need, and whether you want a big brand or you're happy to try a newer, smaller brand. Once you've answered those questions, searching and saving hundreds is a cinch.

It's also one of the easiest bills to switch. You can take your mobile number with you when you move providers, and switch your broadband in a matter of minutes.

But it's one of the toughest to fix when something goes wrong: in my experience most people's telco frustrations are about service and reliability rather than just price.

So here's what you can do about killing telco bills.

Once again, if you're just after a quick saving, try the 'Quick Bill-Kill' below. If you want to learn how to save on telco bills over and over again, read the whole chapter and collect another Bill-Killing Belt at the end.

At a glance

Potential saving	From $50 up to $1000 in some cases.
Degree of difficulty	1 out of 5 (once you know what you want).
Best times to save	Anytime, but ideally when there's just been a leap in the data limits on offer.

Time required to switch	Starting from 15 minutes.
Top online tools	Whistleout.com.au is hands-down the best telco comparison website. There's no government comparison website for telco.
If I could tell you one thing about telco bills it would be:	These products are *constantly* changing. Switch every year or two and you can usually save or get much more for the same amount of money.

QUICK BILL-KILL: Telco

If your mobile plan is lousy value or you have to pick a new broadband package but you're squeezed for time, no sweat. It's never been easier to save between $50 and $1000 p.a. in 20 minutes or less.

Here's a four-step guide to notching up a quick result:

1. **Check your current mobile or broadband plan:** What do you pay each month? What's your data download limit? What's the speed (if it's NBN)? What else is included (Calls? Phone? Modem?) Do you want the same things from a new plan?

2. **Go to whistleout.com.au, Australia's most comprehensive telco comparison site.** These guys are total telco nerds. Enter the info about what you're looking for – limits, speeds, hardware and other inclusions. (Don't know what you need? In that case, this will take a little longer and you should read 'Everything You Ever Wanted to Know' later in this chapter.)
3. **See which plans they recommend.** They might show a couple of 'featured' ones first who pay for the top spot, but then they'll rank the rest from cheapest to most expensive. Most of the cheap ones will be brands you've hardly heard of. Most of the expensive ones you'll know. Ask yourself: does the brand matter? Their mobile network or their NBN 'pipes' are the same as the big guys. The only difference will be the price, the customer service, and maybe the hardware they include. Your call. (I like to go for brands in the middle somewhere – established enough to know their stuff but new enough to be hungry for customers.)
4. **At this point, if you're happy to switch and you don't like haggling, you can just sign up to the plan you've picked.** But if you like your current provider, call them up and tell them about the plan you're thinking of moving to. Ask them to beat it. Telco is super-competitive and they'll probably play ball. Here's that basic script again:

'Hi there, my name is [Robert De Niro/Insert Your Name Here]. Perhaps you could put me through to someone on your retention team to see if they can help? I've been a loyal customer of yours for _______ years and I'd like to stay on, but I've just received a really good offer from another provider and I think it might be a better deal than the one I'm on. _______ has offered me _______. I wondered whether you can match it or even beat it? If you can, I'll lock it in right now.'

Don't forget to tell us about your win! Post your saving to @OneBigSwitchAU and @KillBillsBook with the hashtag #KillBills and we'll share it with all the other Bill-Killers out there.

HARD TRUTH: The one big decision every telco customer needs to make

There are a few things that make those mobile and broadband bills different to every other bill stuck to your fridge.

Here's one of them: Telstra.

When it comes to telco, the first big decision that most Aussies have to make is: to Telstra, or not to Telstra?

No other industry has such a massive concentration of customers with one single provider. The former government monopoly was privatised from 1997 onwards and it still has about half of Aussie telco customers, and many are blindly loyal.

To use some of the ideas we discussed in Part 1 of this book, there are a lot of 'Sleeping Beauties' out there on Telstra plans, and many of us are letting our 'Loss Aversion' and our 'Status Quo Bias' prevent us from saving big bikkies.

Because take it as read: Telstra almost always costs more. So if you're going to pay extra to Telstra, you just need to make sure you have a good reason to (and yes, there *are* some good ones - here are a few examples below).

GOOD REASON #1:	You live or work in regional Oz, in a spot where there's no other viable mobile network, so of course you're prepared to pay more.
GOOD REASON #2:	You still need your landline, for some reason, although mobile plans are now cheaper anyway (and you can take them out with you, Gran!)

GOOD REASON #3:	You're a sports nut who's addicted to getting it all down the Foxtel cable and recording it on your IQ box (although most sport is now accessible by streaming apps owned by the NRL or AFL - or even co-owned by Telstra themselves in the case of Foxtel Now and Kayo).

If you *are* prepared to break up with Telstra, on the other hand, the savings can be significant. In the case study below based on early 2019 prices, 'un-bundling' a Telstra package and making a few compromises can save a household $600 a year.

Case Study: To Telstra, or not to Telstra?

Not that long ago, if you wanted Foxtel sport, a big family internet plan, a big-data mobile plan and a home phone (and a lot of families do), you often paid Telstra more than $250 a month for the privilege. (Some people will still be paying these old prices. Last time I checked, Foxtel's Platinum package alone was $139 a month.)

But by early 2019, thanks to the revolution of streaming services, you could get the equivalent of all that for about $180 from Telstra, albeit delivered in slightly different forms.

And if you were prepared to leave Telstra, you could get the rough equivalent for under $125 a month.

Let's take a snapshot from early 2019 and compare an example of a Telstra bundle to an 'un-bundled' package I put together.

(NB: this industry is constantly changing so these bundles will already be replaced by something else, but you'll get the idea. The value in telco is getting better and better so you gotta shop around once in a while!)

EXAMPLE 1: Telstra bundle

For about $130 a month with a 24-month contract, Telstra was offering:

- unlimited broadband data;
- 50Mbps speed;
- Telstra TV;
- a Telstra modem;
- Unlimited standard local, National and Australian mobile calls; and
- a Foxtel Now Starter package with a Sports upgrade.

New customers were also billed a $99 activation fee.

For a mobile plan, you could get the 30GB Telstra BYO SIM-only plan for $49 per month. (At the time, Telstra didn't discount you for taking both mobile and broadband with them, which is irritating, but some Telstra mobile customers did get access to bonus data or mobile calls.)

TOTAL COST: $179 per month plus set-up fee of $99.

EXAMPLE 2: My home-made 'bundle'

For $70 a month over 24 months, Optus was offering you:

- unlimited broadband data;
- 50Mbps speed;
- a wi-fi modem;
- Internet (VOIP) phone line.

There was also a $99 set-up fee for this one.

For a mobile plan, you could get the 30GB Optus BYO SIM-only plan for $35 per month. (This is the plan I'm currently on. Optus used to give a $20 bundle discount, which is why I took it out, but they'd stopped offering that to new customers at the time of writing.)

If you're a sports fan and reluctant to 'cut the Foxtel cord', consider this: their new Kayo streaming service ('the Netflix of sport') starts from only $25 a month.

If you're a football nut, an Optus Sport package with Premier League Football starts from only $15 a month.

TOTAL COST: $130 per month with Kayo sports, plus the cost of calls from your home phone (which never gets used at my place) and a $99 set-up fee.

THE VERDICT

Telstra costs an extra $50 a month, or $600 a year, compared to a comparable home-made bundle of Optus and Foxtel streaming services.

And that was based on 'new customer prices' in early 2019 - bear in mind that many old Telstra customers are still paying old 'Sleeping Beauty' prices.

If you're still paying some of those old prices for Foxtel and Telstra services, the saving could be more like $1000+ in a year, expecially if you're prepared to try even less-established brands.

If you don't need to pay that extra dough, why would you?

And, as the true story below reveals, sometimes you don't even need to move to a streaming service to slash your Foxtel bill dramatically.

True Story: Richie slashes his Foxtel bill without getting rid of the IQ box

My friend Richie loves his HBO. When I told him I was watching the sixth season of *Game of Thrones* on Foxtel Now's basic package for $15 a month (NB: it's since gone up to $25), he did what hundreds of thousands of Foxtel subscribers are doing lately.

He started to question the value of his $120 a month Foxtel package.

INSIDE INFO: Foxtel knows this and they're scrambling so hard to respond to the invasion of streaming services that they've even launched competitors to their own business in Foxtel Now and Kayo Sports. They'd rather eat themselves than be eaten by others.

Richie was aware of this and he knew exactly who to ask for when he rang them up.

'I called them up and I said, "Look, let's save ourselves 20 minutes. Can you just put me straight through to the Retention Team, please."

'I told the guy my buddy was streaming *Game of Thrones* for $15 a month and he asked me "What is it you really want to watch?".'

'I said, "I want HBO', and he said "We can give you that for $27.90 a month for the next 6 months if you keep the IQ box and stay."'

'So I said, "Done".'

The best insider tricks to use on . . . telco

The Moving Target

As I explained in Part 1, this insider trick is all about bills that change regularly, and how to exploit that movement. And telco plans are the biggest moving target of the lot!

They change faster than any other major household bill, because they're based on new technology – and technology in this area is advancing at warp speed.

Look at it this way. In 2010, Aussies downloaded about 250,000 terabytes of data on our broadband plans. By 2017, that had skyrocketed to over 3.5 million terabytes!

That's a 1300% increase, or *13 times* as many songs, movies, *Game of Thrones* episodes, YouTube cat videos, Google searches, spreadsheets, emails and pouty Instagram selfies as seven years before!

Fortunately, our data plans haven't become 13 times more expensive, and that's because the technology is moving fast enough to keep up with our data obsession: in other words, data is becoming cheaper for the telcos to move, so they're able to give us more and more for about the same price.

Have you ever been offered a free upgrade to your data limit? You should have been. In Part 1, I told the story of how my first ever broadband provider tripled my data limit without asking me for any extra money.

Telco is one of the only industries where providers do sometimes give you more for the same price, but don't wait for the phone to ring. Check in once every year or two to see what the new 'going rate' is.

True Story: How I used the 'Moving Target' trick with my own telco

Two years ago, I was getting 4GB of data on my mobile plan for about $60 a month.

I then took up a mobile deal we negotiated for One Big Switch members and I upgraded to 10GB of data every month for just $40.

This year, the same provider launched a new plan with 30GB of data for just $35! So I moved again, as my 12-month contract had expired.

So do the maths: over the past few years, I've gone from paying $15 per GB of data to less than $1 per GB.

If I hadn't followed the moving target, I'd be paying almost double the amount I'm paying now and probably busting my data cap every time we did a road trip and played Spotify songs all the way up the coast.

KILLER STAT: Australians waste $315 million a year on excess data charges from going over their mobile cap. I wonder how many of them could get that extra data for free if they checked the latest plans available?

David's Slingshot

Here's another thing that's unique about your telco bills. It can be tough to decide what you need: how much data, what speed, and all that.

But once you know what you want, in my opinion, no other household bill is so *easy* to compare and switch online.

Sure, there are some little differences between products, such as sneaky set-up fees and inclusions or exclusions. And there's the whole getting-the-modem-connected challenge when you sign up for a new broadband plan.

But on the whole, every telco provider is selling a similar product, particularly so with mobile providers.

For years now, you've also been able to 'port' your mobile number when you switch, which is a big help when shopping around but still hasn't happened with bank accounts and other bills.

All of these factors have allowed comparison websites to build very powerful online tools where you tell them what you need and they show you your options in a very simple way.

(Compare this to home & car insurance, for example, where insurers refuse to share their prices with comparison sites and therefore these sites only compare a handful of policies. More on that in the next chapter.)

INSIDE INFO: There are only three mobile networks in Australia (Telstra, Optus and Vodafone). Every mobile plan is on one of those three! So it's possible to get a mobile plan on the Telstra network that costs less than the equivalent Telstra plan, and the same applies to Optus and Vodafone. If you're in a well-served area, there may be no good reason to pay extra for a big name. Have a look at some of the brands below that operate on the big-name networks:

Telstra 4G network	Optus 4G network	Vodafone 4G network
Aldi Mobile	amaysim	Hello Mobile
Belong	Catch Connect	Kogan Mobile
Boost Mobile	Coles Mobile	Lebara Mobile
Lycamobile	Dodo	Think Mobile
Pennytel	Exetel	TPG
Southern Phone	Hive Mobile	
Tangerine Telecom	iiNet	
Telechoice	Jeenee Mobile	
Think Mobile	Moose Mobile	
Woolworths Mobile	Spintel	
	Vaya	

So the internet is a vital weapon in your battle against big telco bills. There are some real Goliaths in this industry, and the web really is your slingshot, little David!

If you're not internet-savvy, invite a friend or grandkid over, feed and water them, and point them at the computer.

Start with the comparison website Whistleout.com.au, which is the standout for telco, and you won't look back.

And remember the advice from Part 1 - don't be bamboozled by the number of choices. They're mostly selling the same thing. 'Good enough' is almost always good enough.

The Elizabeth Taylor

This trick is about taking honeymoon offer after honeymoon offer, and never paying the 'Sleeping Beauty' price, as we explained in Part 1.

Because the telco market moves faster than Australia changes prime ministers, it pays to check in whenever your contract expires and see what's available now.

If you've been married to your telco on a contract for a year or two, the telco dating scene will probably look quite different. You'll be like a middle-aged divorcee discovering Tinder for the first time.

And that's why the 'Elizabeth Taylor' works on telco bills - new customers get the best deals, and you can too by taking honeymoon after honeymoon if you're prepared to keep moving.

True Story: My mum saves $120 and gets a new toy

My mum is a natural researcher and she likes to save a few bucks. (That's us at Christmas.)

As she puts it, older people are better at this money-saving stuff 'because we've got the time!'

Last year she called me to say she'd just saved $120 a year on her Telstra NBN with about ten minutes of effort.

It all started when she saw a Telstra offer for new customers on the Whistleout website that was cheaper than she was paying, and included things she wasn't getting.

Well, Grandma Deb was having none of that.

She called Telstra and in no time at all, she'd saved $10 a month, 'plus we got a Google Mini into the bargain'.

The only downside is that when the grandkids visit, they now spend more time talking to Google than they do to their grandma!

Onya, Mum x

The Squeaky Wheel

Aussies have a *lot* of complaints about our telcos. We had 167,831 in the 2017–2018 financial year, to be precise. (That's about one formal complaint to the ombudsman every three minutes.)

This actually came down from past years, when the early rollout of the NBN caused complaints to skyrocket.

As I explained in Part 1 of the book, these are big businesses and your complaint is like one of those little penguins busting a gut to survive in the David Attenborough docos – you need to give it a leg-up.

I've found that the best way to get your telco's attention when there's a problem is to apply the sliding scale approach. First, ask to speak to a manager. If you get no result, then make it public (but polite) on their social media page. Still no joy? Make it official.

The Telecommunications Industry Ombudsman ('TIO' to their mates) is your mate too.

TIO opens a file when you make an official complaint, they give it a number, and they require your telco to open a file and to put someone in charge of resolving it too. Bingo.

Your efforts to get some poor sod in a foreign call centre to fix your problem were valiant, but it was always a longshot. Now you've made your little penguin stand out from the colony.

Here's where to contact your new best mate TIO: www.tio.com.au/making-a-complaint

TIGHTARSE TIP: The other thing many telcos do quite well is live chat. If you can't bear the thought of spending half an hour on the blower with them, try their live chat option first. You can do other things while they get to the bottom of your issue.

True Story: Penny solves her telco problem while getting her grocery shopping sorted

Penny works at the company that published this book and she's something of a Bill-Killer herself.

She told me this great tale about using live chat to sort out a connection problem while she got some other chores done:

'I was having internet connection issues and I'd tried everything to get it to work at home myself.

'I'd been through this before and I knew the consultant would just make me run all over the house unplugging and plugging in things that I'd already tried.

'I loathe sitting on hold, so I'd recently started trying out the "live chat" options at work, toggling between chat and emails to get those pesky "business hours" queries done.

'I was also pressed for time, so I picked up my smartphone, started a live chat session and headed out to the shops.

'As I pushed my trolley along the aisles, every few minutes I'd get a message that said "please do this". So I'd respond with "OK, one sec", grab a few more grocery items and then reply "OK done but still not working".

'Over the next 20 minutes we repeated this exchange several times before they finally agreed with me that there was definitely a problem and they'd send a new unit out.'

How cheeky's that? Shopping done, connection fixed, and no waiting on hold. #winning

5 Other Ways to Save on Telco

1. **Bundle your mobile and internet and pay TV:** Sometimes it works out cheaper if you take more than one product with the same provider. If you're happy with your broadband provider, ask them if they give mobile discounts to their customers. And vice versa with your mobile provider. But note that some providers do and some don't, and sometimes they chop and change so it's hard to predict.
2. **Un-bundle your mobile and internet and pay TV:** I know, I know. Now I'm telling you to do the opposite of what I just told you to do. Annoying isn't it? But here's why: it all depends on the deal. Some bundles are great value, other bundles are not. Sometimes you're better off getting the bits and pieces from different providers (see the case study above for a great example). Sometimes you get real rewards for going all-in with one provider. So work out what's best for you.
3. **Ditch the landline:** Why? Why? Why are you still paying extra for a home phone? This has become one of telco's greatest rorts. If there's a good reason for you to have one, then fair enough. I won't give you a hard time. Good reasons include:
   - 'I have lousy mobile reception.'
   - 'It costs me nothing extra.'
   - 'It works in a blackout whereas home phones that run through the internet do not and I need a

phone that always works because I do not have a mobile.'

- 'I believe mobiles give you cancer/the Chinese government is listening in/other implacable personal opinions.'

But if you *don't* have a good reason, that means you're paying for a service you don't need. By the way, the following are no longer good reasons:

- 'It's cheaper than mobiles.' Actually, it's not anymore – most mobile plans now offer unlimited calls to Australian numbers.
- 'It's expensive to call long distance on mobiles.' Again, not always true. Many cheap mobile plans have low long-distance charges or included long-distance calls in their plans.
- 'I don't want to give the number up.' This is understandable but there are ways around it – you can always divert it to a mobile number for six months, for example, while everyone catches up on your move. This will cost less than the landline.

By the way, once the NBN comes to your home you'll have 18 months until they cut the old copper wire anyway, so most landlines will eventually be disconnected.

4. **Use wi-fi whenever possible:** Whenever you are in a wi-fi network that you have access to, don't use your mobile data. As long as you have wi-fi turned on on your phone, and you've entered the wi-fi password into that phone in the past, it will connect

to the wi-fi network and use wi-fi data not mobile data. So, to give the obvious example . . . use the wi-fi at work instead of your mobile data. Use the wi-fi at the cafe if they have a free network, too. Use the wi-fi anywhere there's wi-fi that's already paid for!

TIGHTARSE TIP: If you've got a home internet plan, you can now use mobile apps such as WhatsApp or Facebook Messenger to call friends and family anywhere for free. Also, if you're a Telstra customer, they've created a widespread wi-fi network out of all the other Telstra customers out there called 'Telstra Air', so make the most of it when you're out and about!

5. **Get a massive data plan on your phone and use that at home instead of broadband:** With mobile providers now offering more than 30GB of data a month for around $40 if you BYO phone, this is a trick being used by more and more people who don't need a lot of data at home. It helps if your plan allows you to 'tether' – this means using your phone as a modem to run other appliances at home such as laptops or desktop computers – and it also helps if certain apps you use a lot, such as streaming apps, are 'unmetered' on your plan, meaning they don't count towards your data limit.

Everything you wanted to know about telco (and then some . . .)

Is Telstra's mobile network better in the bush?

The short answer is yes. All three mobile networks – Telstra, Optus and Vodafone – claim they cover 98% or 99% of Australians but that's the population, not the landmass, and most of us live in the coastal cities. So outside the big smoke, it's often Telstra or nothing at all. But remember that there are other providers that operate on the Telstra network, so you might have some choice – albeit limited. Those other providers don't get access to the full Telstra network, though, so check their regional coverage before you sign up if possible.

Is Telstra better in the cities?

There is now very little difference in metro areas, and it changes from time to time. Sometimes Telstra is fastest, sometimes Optus. Even Vodafone, whose network once saw it nicknamed 'Vodafail', has now built a red-hot 4G network in metro areas. So mostly it depends where you live and work.

If you want to see what each network is like in your area, you can do so by entering an address at each network's coverage page:

TIGHTARSE TIP: German supermarket Aldi has some of the cheapest BYO mobile plans around, and they operate on parts of the Telstra network. So in most of Australia, you can get Telstra coverage at Aldi prices. Woolworths also has mobile plans on the Telstra network, and Coles has plans on the Optus network.

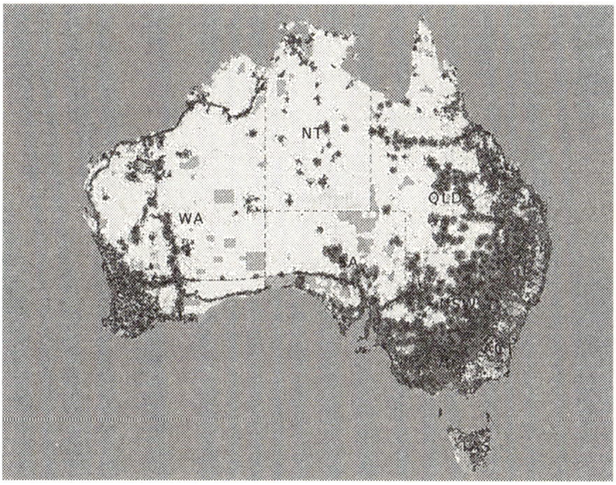

TELSTRA: www.telstra.com.au/coverage-networks/our-coverage

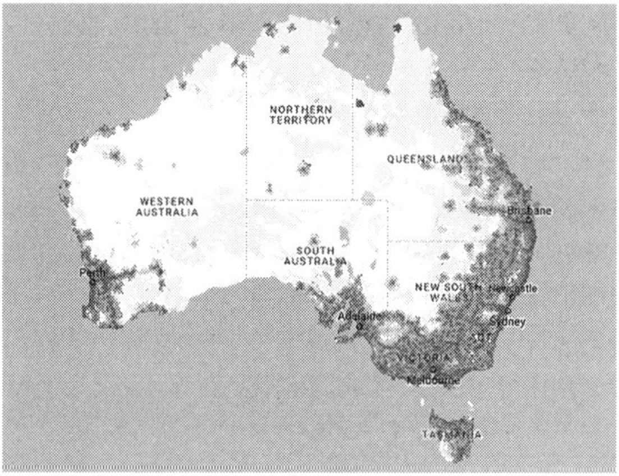

OPTUS: www.optus.com.au/shop/mobile/network/coverage

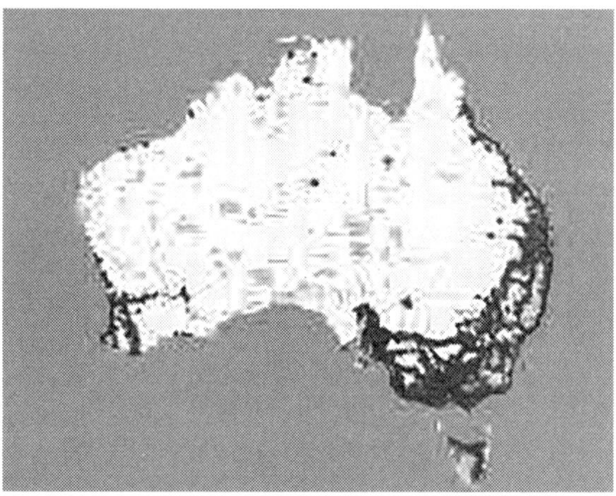

VODAFONE: www.vodafone.com.au/network/coverage-checker
Image source: whistleout.com.au

Who's the fastest fixed-line internet provider?

This changes from time to time, but Telstra topped the charts in most of the tests done in 2018 and 2019. Netflix tests the speed of different providers in prime time, for example, and Telstra's NBN connections came out on top in 2019 at 4.38Mbps (followed by Optus, then Exetel, then Telstra's non-NBN connections). Telstra also topped the Ookla speed test results in late 2018, including in the crucial 7–11pm prime time category when connections slow down due to 'peak hour' online. Second was Optus, then TPG and iiNet. Ookla is an online speed test that anyone can use to see how fast their internet connection is, so these results are based on those who have used the Ookla test online.

How fast is *my* internet?

You can check this anytime for free using the Ookla Speed Test online: www.speedtest.net/

Who's the best at customer service?

There are a few ways to answer this question. One way is to look at how many customers make complaints to our mate 'TIO' (The Telecommunications Industry Ombudsman - see above for more info). Based on recent years' data from TIO, Optus has had the highest proportion of unhappy chappies (measured in complaints per 10,000 connections), but that was probably boosted by their stuff-up streaming the Football World

Cup in 2018. They were followed by Telstra, Vodafone and Amaysim.

Another method is to look at online reviews at sites such as CanstarBlue.com.au or ProductReview.com.au. If you do that, you'll often see brands such as Internode or iiNet featuring near the top – both have historically good reputations for customer service. But as I said in Part 1, treat crowd-sourced online review sites with a grain of salt: they can be gamed because their business model is to make businesses pay a fee to improve their ratings on the site. So the business on top might be paying the website for help in reaching that position, while the ones down below may have merely refused to do so.

A third way is to ask around, which is often the best way. Ask your Facebook friends, for example, who they're with and how they'd rate the customer service.

When is the NBN coming to my place?

The National Broadband Network is rolling out across Australia with the aim to have more than 8 million homes and businesses connected by 2020.

Find out exactly when it's due at your place using the NBN rollout map here (and you can also register to get updates): www.nbnco.com.au/connect-home-or-business/check-your-address

What do I have to do once the NBN arrives?

You'll need to pick a new plan. Once the NBN comes to your address, you have 18 months before the old copper wire that carries old-fashioned ADSL broadband is disconnected.

There's often no cost but do check as there might be an installation or hardware fee. (For instance, if you are installing NBN to a newly built home, NBN charges your provider a $300 service cost.)

NBN is the wholesaler, not the retailer. You can't buy direct from them. You'll need to select a plan with a retailer/ISP (Internet Service Provider).

KILLER STAT: Four out of five of us are just signing onto an NBN plan with our current provider, but this is your chance to save a few bucks – whether you switch or stay, you're a very attractive proposition to telcos when the time comes to make this decision. So take the opportunity to see what else is out there!

I feel the need for speed . . . but which NBN speed?

There are four speed options with fixed-line NBN. It depends what you want to do with it.

NBN Product Name	Speed
Basic NBN 12	12Mbps
Standard NBN 25	25Mbps
Standard Plus NBN 50	50Mbps
Premium NBN 100	100Mbps

Casual, everyday user? Or low budget? The Basic speed might be enough - it's designed to deliver half the maximum speed of an old ADSL plan.

Work from home? Or household of gamers and streamers? Maybe consider the Standard Plus or Premium options, with speeds of 50 or 100Mbps.

(NBN recommends the Standard Plus 50Mbps plan, for what it's worth.)

Why isn't my NBN as fast as claimed?

Traffic on the road slows down at peak hour, and so too does the internet. Many providers are now advertising a more realistic 'evening speed' on their plans, after the consumer watchdog went on the warpath against telcos who were not delivering their advertised speeds at peak times.

Which broadband data limit do I need?

Forty-three per cent of Australians exceed their data plans on a regular basis, according to research from Deloitte, so be realistic. The best guide is your past behaviour, if you've had a plan already. Look at an old internet bill, or log into your account to find out.

Or use an online data calculator like the one at whistle out.com.au: quiz.leadquizzes.com/q/vCiBkr

Or just go unlimited. Large households or big internet users are now turning to unlimited data plans to avoid excess data fees. They no longer cost an arm and a leg, ranging from $50 to $100 a month.

Cable, NBN, ADSL and wireless: what's the difference?

They're just different types of 'pipe' that your internet comes down.

The major difference is the connection between the 'node' (buried under a footpath nearby) and your home. This connection can significantly influence speed and efficiency.

TYPE	WHAT IT MEANS
Cable broadband	Involves running a coaxial cable to the node and then fibre optics from the node to your home - much like a Foxtel connection! Speeds run up to 30 Mbps, however this can slow down the further your house is away from the 'node' and at peak times, when there are more people online.

ADSL or ADSL 2+	Involves running a copper cable from the exchange to the node and then to your home. Speeds run up to 24 Mbps, however, this can slow down the further your house is away from the 'node', and at peak times.
NBN	Involves running fibre optics to the node and then a cable from the node to your house. But average speeds do not slow down the further your house is away from the 'node' and at peak times, because users aren't put into 'group nodes'.
Mobile broadband	No cables! This broadband arrives via a wireless signal on the same 4G network that mobile phones use. In other words, it's the same as the data that you download on your phone.

Collect another Belt, Grasshopper

If you've read the energy and telco chapters from start to finish, you're on a roll and it's time to pick up your next Bill-Killing Belt.

This one is Yellow and you're well on the way to Black Belt status, by which time you'll be a money-saving kung-fu master.

Next we'll tackle home & car insurance, which need to be tackled in a very different way to telco.

CHAPTER 12
CAR & HOME INSURANCE

All up, we pay about $15 billion a year for these products in Australia, at an average of about $600 per policy.

If you have a mortgage, you're required to have home insurance. Most car owners have some form of car insurance. And many of us have contents insurance, whether we're renters or owners.

There's a lot of fat in some insurance premiums, particularly if you're a 'Sleeping Beauty' with one of the big established brands and you've just been dutifully paying the slightly higher premium they send you each year (which is four in five of us, incidentally).

But car and home insurance are stuck in the dark

ages. There's precious little transparency around the price of these products and no way to easily compare them online.

In this chapter I'll explain why that is, and what you can do to get around it.

As usual, check out the short and sweet 'Quick Bill-Kill' if you're stuck for time and you just need a quick saving. Or read the whole chapter to turn yourself into a home & car insurance Bill-Killer *par excellence*.

At a glance

Potential saving	From $100 up to $1000, depending on the value of your car or home
Degree of difficulty	3 out of 5
Best times to save	When your renewal arrives
Time required to switch	From about half an hour per bill – mostly on the phone with your provider.
Top online tools	• your own insurer's website • cheap challenger brands such as budgetdirect.com.au, youi.com.au or woolworths.com.au • consumer clubs such as OneBigSwitch.com.au or RACV, RACQ, NRMA, RAA, RACWA

If I could tell you one thing about home & car insurance bills it would be:	Make sure you're paying the 'New Customer' premium, not the old, 'Sleeping Beauty' premium.

QUICK BILL-KILL: Home & Car Insurance

If your renewal shows a big premium increase and you're stuck for time, here are four steps to a quick and dirty saving on your car or home insurance that takes about half an hour:

1. **Grab your renewal and last year's renewal.** This will reveal much your premium's gone up by (it almost never goes down).
2. **Go to your own insurer's website.** Get an online quote using *most* of the same details as your current policy (use a different address nearby and/or licence plate so you don't confuse their computer, which will probably have yours saved).
3. **Go to one of the 'challenger brand' websites listed above.** (It's up to you which one – they're all pretty cheap as a rule.) Get a quick quote using the same details as the one above.
4. **At this point you can switch or you can call your insurer and tell them about the other offers you've got.** Ask them what they're prepared to offer to keep you. If they don't come to the party, switch! Here's that basic script again:

'Hi, my name's [Groucho Marx/Robert De Niro/Insert real name here] and I've been a loyal customer of yours for ______ years. I've recently received my renewal notice. I couldn't help noticing that it's gone up by _____. And I also couldn't help noticing that it's ______ more than you're charging a new customer with similar details to me. I know this because I got a quote on your website for a new policy with my details and I must have accidentally put my neighbour's address in. Whoops! Anyway, the quote came in at _____. How is that fair? I'd like you to match that new customer price please, and if you can I'll renew right now. If you can't, I've got a quote from another provider and I'm tempted to take my business elsewhere.'

Remember: Tell us about your win! Post your saving to @OneBigSwitchAU and @KillBillsBook with the hashtag #KillBills and we'll share it with all the other Bill-Killers out there.

HARD TRUTH: What the insurance industry doesn't want you to know

When it comes to shopping around, home & car insurance are different to other bills such as energy and telco.

That's because most home & car insurers are determined to make it hard for us to compare their prices, and they've fought tooth and nail to stop it.

While there are about 100 insurers in Australia, a 2016 parliamentary inquiry reported that 'the home and motor insurance market in Australia is dominated by four main insurers - IAG, Suncorp, QBE and Allianz - issuing cover under multiple brands. Collectively, these larger insurers make up approximately 74 per cent of the market'.

For example, IAG owns NRMA, RACV, Coles Insurance, SGIO, SGIC, WFI, CGU and others.

Suncorp owns AAMI, GIO, Bingle, APIA, Shannons, Terry Scheer and others.

The insurance giants are opposed to comparison websites, even though they exist in the UK, Norway, Ireland, the US and that most remote of foreign countries - North Queensland (where the government intervened to build one because it became so hard to get affordable insurance after the cyclones and floods of the last decade).

But for most Australians, there is still no one spot on the internet where you can compare pricing from the majority of insurers.

The industry says that comparing insurance policies based on price will lead us to downgrade our cover without realising it and we could end up underinsured - and they might have a point.

KILLER STAT: According to an Insurance Council of Australia report, one in four Aussie homeowners don't even know what's covered in their policy.

But another of the reasons I suspect they've resisted transparency is that pricing varies widely between the insurers, and particularly between new customers and old 'renewing' customers.

Some of the established big brands would lose a lot of customers if it was easy to see how much more they are charging their 'Sleeping Beauties', compared to what new customers are paying - either with the big brands or the newer, hungrier challenger brands.

The big guys defend themselves by saying that their cover is superior, and sometimes that's true too. But most insurance policies are about 90% identical to each other - it's really only a handful of details that differentiate them.

And once you look closely at those for yourself, you might decide those differences are not worth paying extra for.

True Story: Why you should never take the first offer

Ashley, a doctor from the Southern Highlands in NSW, bought a new car and took out an insurance policy through the car dealership.

It cost him $1450 for the first year.

When he got his renewal, he shopped around and he halved his premium.

He was so excited that he called radio host Alan Jones to tell him about his windfall.

'I went and got a quote for Coles Insurance via the FiftyUp Club and have reinsured the car now for $686,' he told Jones on air. 'Isn't that amazing!?'

Don't take it from me. Take it from this former consumer watchdog!

Allan Fels is a former head of the ACCC. More recently he won the gig with the most longwinded title in Australian government: 'The NSW Emergency Services Levy Insurance Monitor'.

Fels's job sounds like someone who shushes people in the library, but don't be fooled. He is as tough as they come and he really irritated the insurance industry when he compared what the top ten home insurers charged their new customers versus their 'loyal', renewing customers.

He found that, on average, *renewing customers paid a 'loyalty tax'* of 34% more.

He also found that 'quotes range from say $1000 to $2700 for the same house and contents at a specified address'.

'This is what is referred to as a loyalty tax, where consumers are penalised for remaining with a company and their product,' Prof Fels said.

'It seems that like banks and energy companies, insurers count on the loyalty of existing customers to offer discounts to new ones.

'This really translates to a simple message for consumers - don't assume you are getting the best deal with your renewals. Always check the prices of other suppliers, and if your insurer is out of line, go elsewhere.'

Data collected by Fels shows home insurance premiums have risen by about $100 on average from 2014 to 2018.

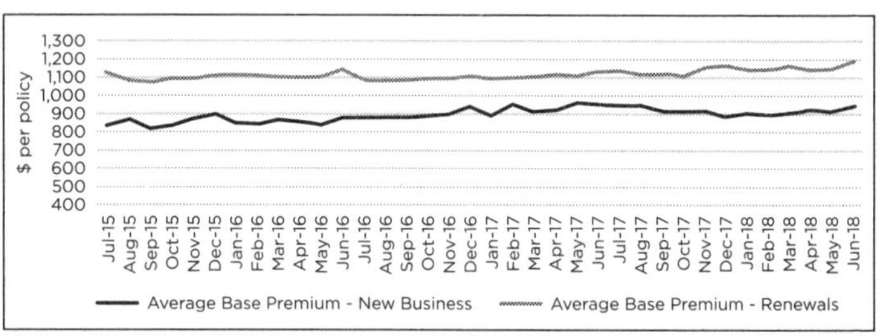

But that's just the average: One Big Switch member Kevin from Nagambie in Victoria wrote to us to say he'd got a 39% increase!

"I just received my home building insurance renewal, [which] went up from $630 last year to $877. What a joke! I will be looking around."

In the industry, this is sometimes known as 'red-lining' - when they give you a premium so high they are basically saying 'Please leave!' (I asked Kevin if he'd made a claim since his last renewal - he said no. Needless to say, he switched providers.)

KILLER STAT: Aussies switched or shopped around on 9.4 million general insurance policies in 2017–18, according to Roy Morgan research. The #1 reason? 'Better premiums'.

NOT-SO-KILLER STAT: 78% of us simply renewed without getting another quote. That's an awful lot of Sleeping Beauties!

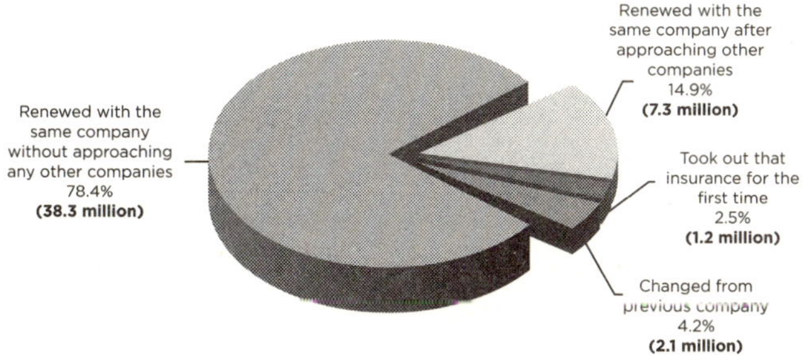

The best insider tricks to use on . . . car & home insurance

The Mystery-Shopper

The key to saving money on your home & car insurance is the ginormous 34% gap between new customer prices and old customer prices.

That's why the 'Mystery-Shopper' is the #1 insider trick you'll need to win the war on this particular household bill.

The 'Mystery-Shopper' involves you donning the disguise of a new customer and seeing whether you get better treatment. If you get better treatment when you look new and shiny, you can use that to demand they treat little 'old' you just the same.

The first 3 steps in my home & car insurance 'Quick Bill-Kill' above use the 'Mystery-Shopper' strategy:

1. Grab your renewal and last year's renewal. This will show you the difference in your new premium. To calculate the percentage increase, use this formula:

$$\frac{\text{(This year's premium minus last year's premium)} \times 100}{\text{Last year's premium}}$$

2. Go to your own insurer's website. Pretend you're a new customer and get a quote using *most* of the same details as your current policy (you might have to 'disguise' yourself with a different address or licence plate as they will probably have yours saved).

TIGHTARSE TIP: Once you get these online quotes, sometimes it pays to wait 24 hours! Some insurers will do what's called an 'abandon cart' offer if you don't accept their quote straight away. So if you've got a day up your sleeve, just wait and see if their offer suddenly improves overnight.

3. Go to one of the 'challenger brand' websites listed above, such as Budget Direct, Youi or Woolworths Insurance. Get a quick quote from them too. They're generally all pretty cheap but if you can't decide, maybe check out the latest star ratings for value at a website such as Canstar.com.au and see who they've rated highly in the past year.

At this point you can switch if you like what you see, or you can give your insurer a chance to keep you.

The Squeaky Wheel

If you're not ready to switch yet, this is where the 'Squeaky Wheel' trick comes in: it's time to have a good old-fashioned whinge.

Remember that the people who work in call centres are human beings too. If someone who regularly paid you money rang up and had a well-researched and polite whinge about the treatment they were getting, you'd probably do your best to solve their problem for them. Most call centre staff are no different - it's a tough job but they get a buzz from helping you out.

So, call your insurer, and politely but firmly tell them how much your premium has gone up by. Ask them why they're charging you more than a new customer. Doesn't loyalty count for anything? Tell them you've got a quote from another provider too (if it's cheaper than your renewal). Ask them what they're prepared to offer to keep you. (There's a full script in the 'Quick Bill-Kill' above.) If they don't come to the party, switch!

True Story: How I haggled a 22% saving on home insurance

A couple of years ago I got my renewal notice from my home & contents insurance provider and the premium had gone up from $1150 to $1216.

It was a 6% increase, so I thought I'd do a bit of 'mystery-shopping'. I went to my insurer's website and entered all my details again, except this time I used my neighbour's address.

This time around, they gave me a new quote for $954. That's a difference of $262 or 22% between what they wanted me to pay and what they were quoting an unknown 'new' customer living next door to me with almost identical details.

So I hit the phones.

> I told the call centre consultant what my Mystery-Shop had uncovered, and they said they couldn't drop my price by that much. But hold on a sec and they'd just speak to their supervisor . . .
>
> A few minutes later they came back on the line and said they could cancel my current policy and create me a new one with the new customer pricing.
>
> So I said go for it.
>
> Morals of the story: never take the first offer; new customers often get better prices; loyalty isn't rewarded; and it pays to whinge politely.

While we're on the subject of having a whinge, remember the escalating steps from Part 1 if you have a problem with your home or car insurer and you want to get a solution in as short a time as possible:

1. First: Whinge (politely) to the boss (in this case, all providers of financial products have to have an internal dispute resolution process so you'll probably be directed to that form).
2. If that fails: Whinge (politely) in public.
3. If that fails: Whinge (politely) to the regulator.

If it gets to step three, you'll need to contact a mob called AFCA.

Since 1 November 2018, all new financial services complaints are dealt with by the Australian Financial Complaints Authority. You can contact them on 1800 931 678 or head to their website: www.afca.org.au

AFCA can conciliate between you and the provider, they can ask for further information to help deal with your complaint, and they can make a decision that's binding on the provider, if it's accepted by you.

You might not be happy with how they've managed a claim, or they might have denied you cover, or given you the wrong information about your policy. Whatever it is, you're not alone and there are people whose job it is to help you out. So do use them!

The Elizabeth Taylor

Insurance is another one of those industries that operates mostly on the 'Honeymoon Strategy' business model: they win new customers over with a very cheap one-year premium and then hope to make money out of you in later years if you don't leave.

Most of us stay, because we couldn't be bothered, and it works for the insurance companies.

But like power companies, it's possible to do an 'Elizabeth Taylor' when dealing with insurers and move regularly, thereby enjoying honeymoon after honeymoon.

Liz married Richard Burton twice, and you might find you leave and later return to the same insurance company - which is fine. Who am I to judge? Or you might threaten to leave and then get retained by a better offer - which is also a win.

Don't worry. It's not like a real marriage. Just go looking for Mr Right-for-Now or Miss Right-for-Now, and if you get a better offer, dump them.

The only possible downside is that some insurers have schemes that reward loyalty, so do make sure you weigh that up against what's on offer elsewhere. Which brings me to the next trick you need to know to ace your insurance ...

The Red Dog

This insider trick is about those rare cases where loyalty *does* in fact pay. To be fair, car & home insurers were one of the first industries to offer rewards for loyal customers.

Multi-policy discounts and no-claim bonuses were early examples of reward and loyalty schemes. These are still offered by some providers, but not all - and they can be valuable.

But do check: don't simply assume you're paying less because you're on one of these policies. Even if you're receiving these bonuses, you might still be paying more.

As the case study on the next page shows, even a 25% multi-policy discount is sometimes more expensive than 'new customer' prices from a challenger brand.

Case study: NRMA's loyalty discounts versus Budget Direct's new customer pricing

NRMA has long been one of the insurers that pioneered multi-policy loyalty discounts.

These days they'll give you up to 25% off some policies if you've been with them for 25+ years and you have 10+ policies (although who has this many insurance policies, I'm not quite sure. John Laws, maybe?)

Let's see whether that discount would make the pricing comparable to quotes from a challenger brand that is very price-focused, such as Budget Direct.

In this case I chose Budget Direct because they've been given an 'Outstanding Value' gong by ratings website Canstar for more than a dozen years in a row, so I know they are likely to be competitive.

I got quotes from both websites using the same details for my own five-year-old Hyundai and the results surprised even cynical old me.

NRMA Comprehensive Car Insurance:

Quote: $1215 (included roadside assistance)

Quote with a 25% loyalty discount applied: $911

Agreed value of car: $7900

Budget Direct Comprehensive Car Insurance:

Quote: $664 (included a 15% discount)

Quote with roadside assistance added: $743

Agreed value of car: $8750

Most of the cover details were very similar. Both offered other 'add-ons' but their exclusions were mostly the same.

INSIDE INFO: Within 24 hours of receiving Budget Direct's quote by email, I received an 'abandon cart' offer from them saying if I took out cover they'd also give me a $60 gift card. So sometimes it pays to wait a day before making a decision . . .

(NB: These are just quotes for my particular details and they don't represent all of NRMA's pricing or Budget Direct's pricing. But they do show that you should never assume you're better off because of a loyalty discount. Do the maths and check to make sure.)

15 other ways to save on car & home insurance

1. **Pay annually, if you can:** Paying by the month is a relatively new phenomenon in insurance and it's becoming more popular, but some insurers will charge you as much as 30% extra over the course of a year for the privilege. It may be difficult to pay a year all at once, but if you can do so, you could save big time.
2. **Raise your excess:** Your 'excess' is the amount you have to pay if you decide to make a claim on your policy. The Insurance Council of Australia explains: 'If your home is damaged in a storm, the

cost of repairing the damage might be $4000. If you had a $600 excess, you'd pay the first $600 and the insurer would pay the remainder.' Most insurance policies have a standard excess that you can increase if you want, which will bring down the regular premium you pay. Excesses can range from about $500 up to $2000.

> **TIGHTARSE TIP:** For a five-year-old Toyota Corolla, increasing your excess by $500 can cut your premium by about $100 a year.

3. **Raise your excess, Part 2:** Most insurers allow you to reduce your premium by electing to pay a higher excess if an accident happens with a driver you *didn't* nominate on your policy. The savings can be around 10–15% and the higher excess is usually around two to three times the standard excess.
4. **You're not locked in!** Contrary to popular belief, you can switch car or home insurance anytime, even if you've paid for the year. There may be a fee but it's usually small, and you're generally entitled to a refund of unused premium. So don't pass up a good deal just because your renewal isn't due yet.
5. **Jewellery and other valuables:** For contents insurance, you usually have to nominate items

valued at over $1000 or a similar amount. If you have a lot of family heirlooms, they could be pushing up your premium substantially. Why not look into the cost of a safe deposit box for valuables you almost never wear, to increase their security and cut the cost of your contents cover?

6. **Younger Drivers, Part 1:** Insuring younger drivers can push up the cost of insurance substantially. If you have to add an under-25 driver to a policy, there are a few ways to minimise the cost. Choose a small car with a small engine, if possible (Young Driver + Big Engine = Big Premium). Choose a locally made car where possible. (Young driver + European Parts = Big Premium.) And if possible, add them to a policy on a new or newish car. Insurance premiums, as a percentage of the value of the car, are significantly lower for new cars – this is based on the common view that young drivers in new cars are a better risk.
7. **Younger Drivers, Part 2:** If you really want to get your premium down, remove younger drivers altogether from the cover. Some insurers allow you to say no one under 25 or 35 or even 50 is going to drive the car, and they'll then drop the price of insurance. This won't go down well if you've got teenage kids! But if they're all grown up, go for it.
8. **Join a group-buying club or savings club:** Membership of a group like One Big Switch or motoring organisations such as the NRMA, RACQ,

RACV, RAA, RAC WA can unlock group-discounted offers on home and contents insurance or car insurance that you can use as a jumping-off point for your research.

9. **Loyalty discounts:** If you've stuck with the same provider for years, then why not call them up and ask for a loyalty discount, even if they don't advertise them? Stranger things have been known to happen.
10. **Use online ratings:** A website such as Canstar.com.au, which rates policies based on their features and price, can be really useful when knowing where to start your research. Canstar looks at 36 different driver and car profiles in six different states to produce its star ratings each year. (In recent years, Budget Direct, Youi and Suncorp have been regular winners.)
11. **Security:** By installing better security (even just locks on your windows or an alarm on your house or car) you can also reduce your insurance premium. Insurers take all these things into account when working out your price.
12. **Conduct a risk assessment:** De-risk your car or home and it could save you on your premium. Clutter, dodgy wiring, overgrown gardens, leaves in the guttering right through to pools and dangerous appliances are all potential hazards, which can lead to a claim and a higher premium. In some cases,

hazards such as a tree near your house will increase your premium, so it might pay to trim it back.

13. **Estimate realistically:** Don't overvalue your personal items and belongings just because of their emotional connection to you. The bigger the price tag you put on them, the more you pay in coverage. Many insurers have a 'house and contents value estimator' on their website, but I'm a bit suss about these tools. Your contents always seem to come out at a higher value than you expected. Which means you pay the insurance company more to cover them. And who created the estimator tool? The insurance company! Funny about that.
14. **Drive less, pay less:** Certain insurers now have policies designed for customers who drive very little. If you tell these insurers your average car usage, they may be able to lower your premium.
15. **Prove you're a good driver:** If you complete a certified 'advanced driving course', some insurers will lower your premium (especially if you're young). These courses last about four to five hours and are a good idea: you'll learn how to brake suddenly, how to handle high speed and dangerous conditions, and you might even have a bit of fun. Also, some insurers now use GPS devices to see how good a driver you are: if you don't mind 'Big Brother' checking up on you, they monitor data on your speed, distance travelled and braking.

Everything you wanted to know about car & home insurance (and then some . . .)

Why does my premium go up every year?

There are a few reasons for this. First, the insurer might be increasing the amount you're insured for each year because the cost of rebuilding a home rises slightly each year with inflation, for example. Second, their costs may be increasing - there might have been a spate of claims in your area or you might have made a claim. And third, they want to make more money out of you, of course! And they're hoping you'll just pay up.

> **INSIDE INFO:** Insurance companies reportedly employ actuaries to estimate by how much they can raise your premium before you'll leave them. Don't let the actuaries win! If you get a big increase, question it using the tricks you've learned in this book.

Why do I get a different price every time I get a quote?

Home and car insurance prices are discriminatory by nature. They're what's called 'risk-based' insurances. Your premium depends on your details: your age, your gender, where you live, your driving or claims history, and your car or home or possessions. It's worked out by complex mathematical algorithms. But every provider has a different algorithm and a different type of customer they are targeting, so prices can vary widely. That's why it's *vital* you don't take the first offer when it comes to these household bills.

How much should I insure my house for?

This is a tough one. Most of us aren't builders. We don't automatically know what it'd cost to rebuild our home or replace our car. But don't just take a stab in the dark. After the 'Black Saturday' Victorian bushfires of summer 2009, an estimated 13% of homes which required reconstruction or significant repair weren't adequately insured, according to ASIC Moneysmart. And many of those who lost their homes in the Sydney bushfires of 2013 were also unable to rebuild them because they didn't have sufficient coverage.

The insurance industry recommends a calculator created by real estate data company Core Logic, which I think looks pretty reliable: understandinsurance.com.au/calculator/building-calculator

If you live in a danger zone and want total peace of mind, consider taking out what's known as a 'Total Replacement Policy', where the insurer agrees to repair or rebuild your home to its current standard. It might be a little dearer. Your call.

How much should I insure my car for?

This is also a tough question but there's lots of help available online. A website such as Redbook (www.redbook.com.au/) will tell you the average trade-in and private sale value of your car.

Most insurers will suggest a 'market value' when you get a quote, based on the car details you give them. *Check it!* Sometimes they get the price down by insuring your car for way less than its *real* market value.

You then need to decide whether to insure it for their 'market value' or an 'agreed value', which is an amount *you* suggest. If you're confident you know what the real value is, or what you're happy to receive if the car is written off, this can be a good option for you.

What's 'Comprehensive' Car Insurance?

This is a high level of insurance that covers not only your own vehicle but that of the other person with whom you've had an accident. It lets you insure your car at an agreed value or its current market value. It's good for valuable cars, or just for total peace of mind.

What's 'Third-Party Property' Insurance?

This is a basic policy that covers damage your car causes to other people and their property, if you have an accident. According to ASIC Moneysmart, some third-party property policies include an 'uninsured motorist extension' that covers you if your car is damaged in an accident and you're not at fault. Check the PDS (Product Disclosure Statement). It's good for cheap 'runabout' cars.

What's 'Third-Party Property (Fire & Theft)' Insurance?

This is third-party property insurance, but with the added benefit of covering your own car for fire or theft. It's good for cheap cars if you want more than the bare minimum cover.

What about all these 'special features' they're offering me?

They're the insurance equivalent of the McDonald's upsell: 'Do you want fries with that?' Many providers offer these as additions to the standard cover, and if you want to keep your costs down you could maybe do without them.They can include burnout of electric motors, accidental damage, public liability and windscreen cover. In the end, the rule is the same as it is with ALL insurance: you've got to decide what's useful to *you* based on your lifestyle and what's a waste of money.

Here is a list of eight popular 'upsells' and what they cover:

1. Flood cover – is defined as the covering of normally dry land by water that has escaped or been released

from lakes, rivers, creeks or other natural watercourse. If you need flood cover, make sure you take up a policy that includes it, or buy it as an add-on.

2. Personal possessions – this covers those everyday valuable items such as mobile devices and jewellery that you sometimes carry around with you. They might already be covered by your policy in the car or home, but in some cases, these high-valued items can also be covered when you're away from the home as an add-on.
3. Accidental damage – a popular extra for those with young kids or grandkids! Most policies only cover damage from so-called 'insurance events', such as fire, explosion, theft or malicious damage (but not backyard cricket, for example). Most policies will not cover accidental loss or damage, except as an add-on.
4. Home emergency – entitles you to have an on-call tradesperson come to your rescue and fix that leaky shower pipe or blocked toilet.

5. Motor burnout cover - aka fusion damage cover. This covers you when the motor in household appliances such as your fridge, freezer or washing machine dies. A power surge or lightning strike can cause this, but do you think it's likely enough to pay extra for? It's up to you.
6. Windscreen cover - this reduces the cost of having a windscreen fixed if it gets chipped or cracked (which is common on open roads). Fixing a windscreen chip can cost about $200 and replacing a whole windscreen can cost over $1000 depending on the make of the car. So it's not a bad idea if you're driving on open roads.
7. Roadside assistance - probably one of the more useful 'up-sell' items, unless you already have it from the manufacturer or dealer or a motoring club. Most new cars rarely break down but when they do, these guys are a godsend.
8. Hire car cover - covers the costs related to hiring a car while your car is under repair or out of action. Do you really need it? It depends on your circumstances. Sometimes it's included as standard anyway.

Do I have flood cover?

Again, you've gotta check! Don't assume anything where insurance is concerned. This is not standard on all policies and usually adds to the premium if you require it. Read the PDS, as they say in all the legalese!

(These are actually not as confusing as they once were, promise.)

What exactly does flood cover include?

Good question. People have been left high and dry in the past because of disagreements over the definition of what a flood is. Many of the Brisbane flood victims of 2011 found they were not fully covered for flood, leading the federal government in 2012 to introduce a standard definition of 'flood' to help establish greater certainty for both insurers and policyholders. The newish industry-wide definition of flood is now: 'The covering of normally dry land by water that has escaped or been released from the normal confines of: any lake, or any river, creek or other natural watercourse, whether or not altered or modified; or any reservoir, canal or dam.' The Insurance Council of Australia says the difference between 'storm' and 'flood' damage is now clear: 'The storm might fill the river, but once the river overflows, that's a flood.'

Collect your Orange Belt, Grasshopper

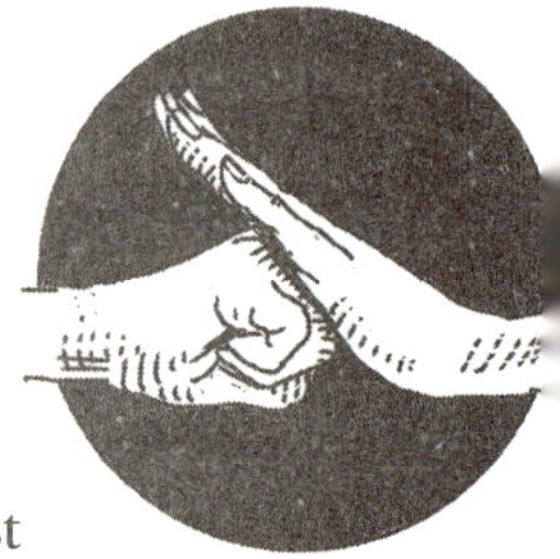

If you've now read the energy, telco and home & car insurance chapters from start to finish, you've earnt three Bill-Killing Belts. This one's Orange, just like stage three in karate (but this book's in black and white so you'll just have to take my word for it).

Just like karate, each belt is a bit harder to earn than the last one, and now it's time to tackle a bill that scares the Bejesus out of most of us but is actually not as intimidating as it seems: health insurance.

CHAPTER 13
HEALTH INSURANCE

I blame the government.

Governments are lousy at building things, but they're even worse at 'half-building' things, and that's what they've done to private health insurance in Australia.

The federal government has bankrolled this industry to the tune of $6.5 billion a year in rebates to take some pressure off the public health system. But in the process they've stitched together a Frankenstein's monster of rules and regulations that very few people really understand.

Millions of us are more or less forced to take out a policy by a convoluted hodgepodge of 'sticks and carrots' in the tax system. So we have to get our heads around this one or it can cost us thousands of unnecessary dollars a year.

The worst thing you can do when it comes to the rising cost of health insurance is to do nothing at all. It really is not as hard as it looks to save hundreds of dollars here, and there are plenty of ways to do so.

The key is not to do it all yourself: to kill this bill, chances are you're going to need some help.

Read the short 'Quick Bill-Kill' below if you just need a result ASAP. But read this whole chapter if you want to know all about how health cover works and how many different tricks there are to keep this bill under control.

At a glance

Potential saving	From an easy $200 up to about $1500 on some higher level policies.
Degree of difficulty	3 out of 5
Best times to save	Just before prices rise on 1 April each year.
Time required to switch	Starting from 30 minutes, but you'll want to consult family members before making a final call.

Top online tools	• commercial comparison sites such as iSelect.com.au or CompareTheMarket.com.au or MembersOwn.com.au • the government website privatehealth.gov.au • group-buying clubs such as OneBigSwitch.com.au or motoring clubs such as NRMA, RACV, RACQ, RAA & RACWA
If I could tell you one thing about Health Insurance Bills it would be:	You're not locked in. The waiting periods you've served are 'portable' and there's probably a similar policy out there for less.

QUICK BILL-KILL: Health Insurance

If your premium is going up again and you're questioning the value of private health insurance, start by making sure you're not paying too much for it.

Here's my four-step guide to a quick saving on your premium:

1. **Look your policy up and down.** Does it still fit or is it like that old pair of stretched undies you should have binned years ago? Do you still need the same

cover? Can you get rid of anything, such as pregnancy cover? Or do you need to add something, such as hip and knee replacements?

2. **Now you're ready to see what else is out there.** Health insurance is not one of the easiest bills to compare so don't be a hero! Use a free comparison service. Go to iSelect.com.au (which covers a range of health funds) or MembersOwn.com.au (which specialises in not-for-profit funds). They require a phone number and they'll call you anyway, so just cut to the chase and call them). Tell them what you need and see what policy they recommend.
3. **Now wait!** Don't accept their recommendation on the spot. Ask them to email it to you. Go to the provider's website and see if they have a special offer available on that policy. These can include 'One Month Free' or 'Six Weeks Free', gift cards valued from $100 to $550, and even discounts of up to 12 per cent. Sometimes they're only for members of certain groups such as motoring groups and consumer clubs.
4. **At this point, you can switch to the policy you've chosen or phone your current health fund and tell them you've got one foot out the door.** Some funds will give you a discount on the spot just to stay, and most will try to find a way to keep you. For example, ask them about 'contribution groups'

or increasing your excess to the maximum amount. Here's that basic script again:

'Hi there, my name is [Robert De Niro/Insert Your Name Here]. I've been a loyal customer of yours for _______ years and I'd like to stay on, but I've just received a really good offer from another provider and I think it might be a better deal than the one I'm on. _______ has offered me _______ . I wondered whether you can match it or even beat it? If you can, I'll lock it in right now. Perhaps you could put me through to someone on your retention team to see if they can help?'

Remember to tell us about your win, too. Post your saving to @OneBigSwitchAU and @KillBillsBook with the hashtag #KillBills and share it with all the other Bill-Killers out there.

HARD TRUTH: Why your health fund is nervous

Until about the last decade or so, health funds were on a very good wicket indeed.

The government would pretty much force people to take out a policy around the time they turned 30 or started earning good money, and then less than one in 20 of them would change funds each year. Jackpot!

But then the Baby Boomers started getting older and claiming more on their policies, premiums went up 18 years in a row, and this became one of the top two most stressful bills for Aussie households, according to CHOICE's quarterly polling.

KILLER STAT: A $2500 policy in the days of Kevin Rudd PM rose to over $4000 in the days of Scott Morrison PM, thanks to two decades of premium increases.

Our ageing population and the increasing cost of whizz-bang medical technology is costing health funds a fortune and they've passed a lot of it on to their customers.

This situation has made the industry more competitive than ever - they're fighting to win customers from their rivals and to stop their own customers from chucking it in.

And that's a good thing for you! Health funds will now play ball if you call them up and say 'I'm thinking of dropping my cover or switching to a cheaper offer'.

What they know that a lot of their customers *don't* know is this: it's easier to switch than it looks. And you've *never* had more help available.

There are all sorts of 'portability provisions' the government has put in place to make switching simpler - for example, you don't have to start over when it comes to waiting periods. You can 'take them with you' if you switch to similar cover, just like you can take your mobile number when you switch telcos.

There's also a new rule that categorises all new policies as Basic, Bronze, Silver or Gold, so they're easier to compare (this will apply to all policies by April 2020).

And there are now all sorts of free websites and businesses that help you to switch, and they've become pretty good at doing the comparisons for you. They're like the mortgage brokers of health insurance, and you'd be nuts not to use them to your own advantage.

The best insider tricks to use on . . . health insurance

The De Niro

There's a lot of blind loyalty in health insurance. To use the corporate jargon we looked at in Part 1, a lot of us are 'Sleeping Beauties', peacefully snoring away while our premiums rise year after year.

Only about 5% of policyholders switch health funds each year, compared to about 20–25% of energy bill payers.

Why don't people shop around more? It looks hard! There are hospital and extras policies, they have confusing names, they're just different enough to make them hard to compare, and then there's a maze of government rewards and penalties as the cherry on top.

And because it's about your family's health instead of your car or your power bill or your dog, you're more afraid than usual of making a bad call. It really plays into those human traits of 'Loss Aversion' and 'Status Quo Bias' that I explained in Part 1 of this book.

So the first insider trick you need to get your head around if you want to win the war on this bill is the De Niro. You need to muster the 'cojones' to walk away from your current policy if it's not doing it for you.

This can be tough. For some of us, it's up there with changing your mortgage provider for difficulty and fear-factor. But you don't need to do it on your Pat Malone. There are smart ways to go about it, and I'm here to tell you what they are.

The key is to keep it simple. If you were hiring a tradie, would you get a quote from everyone in the Yellow Pages? Of course not. You'd get three quotes and you'll have a good basis for a solid decision.

Health insurance is not so different. Soon every new policy will fit into one of four broad categories: Gold, Silver, Bronze, Basic, so get a couple of other quotes on policies in the same category and you'll be on track to find a saving.

True Story: Martin leaves his health fund after 30 years of staying loyal

One of the best things a One Big Switch member has ever sent us was a letter that Martin Doyle wrote to the CEO of his old health fund when he finally decided to switch after about 30 years. Here it is, reproduced with permission from Martin:

01.05.2015

Dear Sir,

I am writing to you today to express how sad I feel to be leaving.

I have been a loyal member since the early 1980s and in that time have held top cover over the years until very recently when I drew back my cover premium to Basic Hospital and Top Extras.

The final straw for me was your offering to your members for a free annual dental check, but only by an approved provider. I have had the same dentist for a number of years, so it is highly unlikely that I, and I'm certain many members, would change dentist for a free yearly check-up. Ask your partner to change hairdresser or barber for a free annual haircut and I'm sure you will get an appropriate response!

Loyalty is about recognising your members

and it's sometimes the small gestures that bind the threads together.

I have now been swayed by One Big Switch. I made a five-minute call yesterday, secured a new policy cover quote which more than equals my current policy cover and I will also be getting a generous cash bonus from making the switch!

A follow-up call today efficiently confirmed all details to switch and begin this relationship.

I am sorry to be parting ways, having invested so many years with you. However I now look forward to moving to a provider that was actually prepared to fight for my business and am looking forward to that new relationship.

Best regards,

Martin Doyle

PS: I hope this letter actually reaches your desk.

David's Slingshot

This is the name I give to the kitbag of internet tools that are making us more powerful as consumers than we've ever been before.

The internet is your saviour when it comes to tackling a big health insurance bill, so get online. If computers just aren't your thing, that's ok – invite someone around who is computer-literate and point them at the keyboard!

There are three main Slingshots you can use to save on this:

Slingshot #1: Use commercial comparison websites. They don't contain ALL health funds but they're very good at what they do

This was one of the first household bills to spawn commercial comparison websites because they could see it was getting more expensive, it was confusing, and people needed help.

KILLER STAT: iSelect, a $160 million Aussie company, was built on the back of people's need for help when picking a health insurance policy!

So whether it's iSelect or HealthInsuranceComparison or CompareTheMarket or MembersOwn, use them! They all know their stuff, it's a free service as long as you're willing to give your number, and while you *will* have to spend some time on the phone with them (they'll only show you plans once you've given them your phone number), you'd be brave to try and tackle this bill solo.

Here's the thing, though. You *don't* have to buy through them. You should use them as a research tool, ask them to email you their results, and only buy through them if they present the best option.

Slingshot #2: Use the government website privatehealth.gov.au (but DON'T SAY I DIDN'T WARN YOU!)

Remember what I said earlier about things that are built by the government?

It was American ratbag writer P.J. O'Rourke who said that 'Giving money and power to government is like giving whiskey and car keys to teenage boys.'

This website is the technological equivalent of a drunken car crash. It's very clunky and hard to use.

But it *does* claim to have every plan on the market and it does help you see what category each plan falls into. It also has some data on the various funds such as what they pay out, how many complaints they get and so on. So you can use it if you need any of that info, but again: don't say I didn't warn you.

Here's my at-a-glance summary of the difference between government and commercial websites on health insurance:

WEBSITE	PRO	CON	GOOD FOR
Commercial comparison websites (iSelect, MembersOwn, etc)	Does a lot of the work for you. Can filter 1000s of options so you're not overwhelmed.	Requires a phone number. Does not contain every provider and every offer on the market.	People who want some help doing comparisons. People who don't mind giving their phone number over.
The government comparison website (PrivateHealth.gov.au)	Contains (almost) all policies on the market. Gives a one-page summary of each policy to simplify the jargon.	Clunky to navigate, and sometimes out of date. Can be confusing; shows you *all* options instead of recommending a plan.	People who are confident doing their own comparisons. People who don't like giving their phone number over.

Slingshot #3: Use the internet to avoid gap payments

Yep, it's the #1 most irritating thing about health insurance: gaps!

You pay your premium month after month, you hardly ever claim, and then when you do . . . there's still a bloody great out-of-pocket payment that averages about $250 but can be thousands for certain procedures.

The gap is the difference between what the health fund covers and what the specialist or hospital charges. You may not be able to avoid them altogether but you can minimise them by shopping around among hospitals or specialists online. Here's how:

1. **Hospital Fee Gaps:** Many hospitals have agreements with Health Funds to cover gaps entirely or partially (on top of any exact excess or co-payment you've agreed to pay when you took out your policy).

   Check which hospitals have a deal with your fund on the federal government website before you decide where to have a procedure: www.privatehealth.gov.au/dynamic/agreementhospitals.aspx
2. **Medical Fee Gaps or Doctors' Fee Gaps:** Some doctors also have agreements with certain funds to cover some or all gaps. It could be a 'no gap' deal or a 'known gap' deal, which caps the gap at a certain amount.

   Check which doctors have a deal with your fund at the government website before you pick a specialist: www.privatehealth.gov.au/dynamic/gapdoctors.aspx

If your fund does *not* have a deal with the hospital and doctor you are planning to use, you have three options:

1. Change hospitals (your doctor might be prepared to do this).
2. Change doctors (your GP or health fund might recommend another specialist). OR
3. Change funds (but make sure you won't have to serve any new waiting periods for your procedure).

TIGHTARSE TIP: According to Bupa, just using your fund's preferred providers for extras claims such as dental, optical, physiotherapy and chiropractic treatments can save a family about $600 a year.

3. Shop around for specialists: Most of us simply use the specialist recommended by our GP, but what if they just chose them because they play golf or went to university together?

Technology is now making it easier to compare the prices and performance of specialists too.

New 'Doctor Review' websites such as www.healthshare.com.au/ and www.whitecoat.com.au/ are displaying more info about specialists' fees and patient ratings to make it easier for others to choose their own specialist if they want to.

Health funds such as NIB, HBF and HCF also have agreements with these websites to give their members access to extra information - so ask them about it.

As journalist Bek Day's story below shows, shopping around for a cheaper specialist could save you as much as $4000 on a single operation.

True Story: Bek saves $8000 over two years with health insurance savings hacks

I told you earlier about my friend and colleague Bek Day, who's made a bit of a name for herself finding health insurance savings hacks and publishing them where she works at kidspot.com.au and news.com.au. I'll let her explain to you how she did it:

'I would conservatively say I have saved about $8000 on my health insurance in two years by customising and streamlining my policy and shopping around for medical practitioners who offer a service.

'One occasion was when my husband needed an operation on his nose. We were facing a $4500 out-of-pocket cost, and with research I managed to avoid paying anything.

'When I spoke to our fund, they explained it was because the specialist was charging *five times* the Medicare Schedule Fee. They told me about a website called Healthshare, where you can search for a doctor in your area who performs the procedure you need with either no gap (no out-of-pocket expenses) or a "known gap" (a maximum of $500).

'Within a week we saw a doctor in our area, told him the other quote was far too expensive, and he agreed to do the surgery for a 'known gap' of $500.

'Another really simple one is to find out what your hospital excess is. When I phoned up to enquire about how I could save on my policy, I was informed that by increasing my excess to $500, I would save $50 per month on my policy. This means a saving of $600 a year, for only a $50 increase in the excess – which I only need to pay if I go to hospital. So far, touch wood, I haven't needed hospitalisation, which means in the two years since discovering this, I've saved our family $1200.

'There are all sorts of ways you can reduce the costs associated with your private health insurance, not only when you need a procedure, but on your monthly premiums as well. A lot of people don't know about this - or, perhaps, don't know where to start - which is why I'm so passionate about educating people on the topic.'

Under-the-Table Deals

There's not a lot of discounting in this industry. In fact, there's a government-regulated CAP on discounts of 12 per cent! (Thanks for nothing, Canberra . . .)

But one of the best-kept secrets in health insurance is a handy little lurk known as 'contribution group discounts'.

There's a weird little loophole in the law that allows health funds to create groups of people and give them all an ongoing discount up to that 12% cap.

That means 'contribution group' members can save up to $480 on a typical $4000 family premium! Although most of the discounts seem to fall into the 4–8% range.

It was created many, many years ago to allow company-wide corporate discounts and that sort of thing, but these days it's being used by everyone from uni staff to government employees to motoring clubs and consumer clubs.

INSIDE INFO: Some health funds now use the 'contribution group' loophole to keep people who are threatening to leave. They've effectively created a special group for their De Niros!

If your fund has a contribution group available to your workplace or a club you belong to (or maybe just to anyone who asks), see if they'll put you in it. It never hurts to ask.

Here are some examples of recent contribution group offers and other under-the-table deals I've seen from motoring clubs and group discount clubs:

NSW: The NRMA has a 7.5% discount for members with Australian Unity.

WA: RACWA has a 5% discount for members with HCF.

SA: The RAA has a 5% discount for members with HCF.

NATIONAL: One Big Switch, where I work, has regular special cashback offers with HCF.

NATIONAL: 9Saver also has regular special offers with Bupa and NIB.

The Squeaky Wheel

If you've got a beef with your health fund, there's help at hand.

Remember the three steps to a successful whinge from Part 1? First, whinge to the boss. If that fails, whinge in public. And finally, whinge to a regulator.

The regulator in this case is called the Commonwealth Ombudsman.

NB: if your beef is with a hospital or a doctor, chances are you need to speak to the health care complaints body in your state or territory. But if it's with your health fund, the ombudsman is the place to go.

The service is free and they're independent and impartial - which means they're not on anyone's side, including yours. 'We do not represent consumers, insurers, hospitals or health services,' they say on their website at www.ombudsman.gov.au/How-we-can-help/private-health-insurance

Complaints about private health insurance peaked in 2016–17 and have since started coming back down. Mainly, people complain about unexpected exclusions and restrictions in their policies - which is why you need to know what you're covered for (and what you're not) before it's too late.

Another common complaint is delays in releasing customers who switch - some health funds will dither in the hope that you'll change your mind.

7 other ways to save on health insurance

With premiums soaring since about 2005, millions of Australians have had to find ways to cut the cost of this bill. Besides switching, there are a bunch of other tricks to get the price down without dropping your cover altogether:

1. **Give Your Cover an Annual Check-up:** Are you finished having children and still paying for obstetrics cover? Are you fit as a fiddle and paying for gastric banding cover? If you don't know the answer, you're not alone . . . Many of us haven't reviewed our policy in years and could be paying hundreds extra for cover we don't need.

   Just keeping it relevant can save you money as you move from one life-stage to another. You can get a summary of your policy from your provider's website, or at privatehealth.gov.au. You can also ask your provider for a history of what you've claimed in the past year - to see whether you're on the right plan.

   Removing obstetrics, IVF and pregnancy services from a policy saves about $500 p.a. for a family, on average. Some funds offer high-level covers without IVF or pregnancy, while some do not. Ask your fund if they do, or use the expertise of a comparison service.
2. **Increase your Excess:** As with all insurance, if you're willing to agree to pay a higher 'excess' when

you go to hospital, you can get your premium down by hundreds of dollars.

For health insurance, 'an excess is an amount that you agree to pay towards the cost of hospital treatment, in exchange for lower premium costs'.

You may be required to pay an excess every time you go to hospital, or only the first time each year – it depends on the policy. But if you're not a regular visitor to hospital, a higher excess might be a good option for you to save some money.

TIGHTARSE TIP: The maximum excess allowed increased from $1000 to $1500 on 1 April 2019 (or $500 to $750 if you're a single). See what would happen to your premium if you paid the higher amount: increasing your excess can often save a family over $500 and sometimes over $1000 on their premium in a year.

3. **Use your Extras!** If you have an 'Extras' policy, it costs you nothing to claim as often as possible on things like dental, optometry, physio and so on. So do it . . . get a massage that's classified as a 'remedial massage' from a therapist who's registered with your health fund. Go to a dentist who's covered entirely by your fund, or who at least has a deal with

your fund to minimise your out-of-pocket costs. And make sure you get a pair of glasses every year.

INSIDE INFO: If you've got health insurance, you may never have to pay for sunglasses again! Here's why. If you have any sort of prescription, even 19:20 vision, you can claim for a pair of prescription sunglasses on many extras policies.

So get a free eye check (it's covered by Medicare), and if the optometrist prescribes any sort of eyeglasses, no matter how subtle, you'll probably be able to order prescription sunglasses and claim them on your extras policy.

I have an annual limit of around $200 for optometry, so every other year I get a new pair of sunnies. No gap!

4. **Pay annually:** If you pay annually before 1 April, when all health funds raise their premiums, you pay the *old* price for the coming year and you effectively postpone the price rise for 12 months. Good trick, if you can afford it.
5. **Pay by direct debit:** Some health funds such as NIB, GMHBA and Australian Unity also offer discounts of up to 4% for paying by direct debit, so consider it.
6. **Who gets the Gong?** If you want to dig really deep, awards can be helpful to weed out the best

value funds and policies. Comparison site Canstar's annual national health insurance ratings are published at this link, for example: www.canstar.com.au/star-rating-reports/health-insurance/ Bupa, HCF and Medibank were the national award winners in 2018 but check the latest results.

7. **Compare the data** (strictly for the health insurance nerds out there, like me): If you're determined to dig deeper and deeper, there is a page on the government website for each fund that shows their 'Performance', including how much they return to members ('Benefits as a percentage of contributions') and their 'Member retention' percentage: www.privatehealth.gov.au/dynamic/insurer

Everything you wanted to know about health insurance (and then some . . .)

Why do I find health insurance so bloody confusing?

Because you're a human being! This is a product that has grown up alongside the public health system and Medicare and covers some health treatments but not others, and some bills but not others, and then the government has gone and made it twice as muddled by adding a long list of tax 'sticks and carrots' to make over-30s and higher income earners take out a policy. The result is something very confusing to the average Joe or Joanne. According to Roy Morgan research,

44% of members find it difficult to understand what their health insurance covers them for.

Doesn't Medicare already provide free health insurance for everybody?

Sort of. Medicare and the public health system cover a lot of health treatments, such as GP visits, emergency departments and public hospital procedures.

We have a universal, free public hospital system and Medicare is one of the best healthcare systems in the world.

But it doesn't cover the following, so if this sounds like you, you'll have to consider private cover:

- You want to choose your own doctor for any elective surgery or hospital visits;
- You want your own room if you have to go to hospital;
- You want to choose which hospital you go to for elective surgery;
- You want a procedure which is 'not clinically necessary' such as cosmetic surgery;
- You want to choose your own dentist;
- You want ambulance cover in certain states; or
- You want cover for 'allied health services' such as dental, physio, optometry or podiatry.

More info here: www.privatehealth.gov.au/healthinsurance/whatiscovered/

What does health insurance NOT cover?

There are two types of policy: Hospital cover and Extras cover. The Hospital policy covers you for treatment as a private patient in a private hospital or a public hospital - it helps cover the cost of in-hospital treatment by a doctor of your choice, accommodation in hospital and theatre fees for surgery. But it does not cover visits to the GP or to many other specialists outside of hospital.

The Extras policy covers 'allied health services' outside hospital such as dentists, optometrists and physiotherapists. But since April 2019 it no longer covers many alternative therapies such as aromatherapy, homeopathy and iridology.

Do I need private health insurance?

Nobody 'needs' private health cover as such, but you have to make your own call about whether you want it. There are three things to consider here: your health, your tax status, and your general attitude to risk.

Firstly, if any of the health matters listed above are quite important to you, then you might want some private health insurance. Or you might have a particular condition that pretty much requires it.

Secondly, for some people the tax system makes it just as expensive *not* to have cover, because you pay extra tax if you don't have a hospital policy (more detail on that below). If that's you, you might as well take out private cover.

Thirdly, you need to decide if you're someone who is prepared to pay for total peace of mind, or would rather play the odds and save the cash (or put it in a bank account and 'self-insure' in case anything major happens).That one's a very personal decision, and it's a decision you need to make with all of your insurances.

How do the government penalties and incentives work?

In the 1990s, the Howard government decided to 'encourage' more of us to take up private health cover to take pressure off the public system.

They used a system of 'sticks and carrots' including the following:

Carrot: The 'Private Health Insurance Rebate', which means the government covers up to 34% of your premium, depending on your age and income,

Stick: The 'Lifetime Health Cover Loading' means that if you don't take out cover by the year you turn 31, you'll pay an extra 2% premium for every year you put it off. (For example, leave it until you're 40 and you'll pay an extra 20% if you want to take out cover.)

Stick: The Medicare Levy we pay at tax time goes *up* if you don't have a private hospital insurance policy and you earn above a certain income (currently $90,000 for a single or $180,000 for a household).

In April 2019, another carrot was added:

Carrot: Discounts for younger people. Take out private health insurance between the ages of 18 and 29 and you'll get a 2% discount for every year you're under 30, up to a max of 10 per cent (For example, take it out at 25 and you'll get a 10% discount.)

Pretty simple, huh? Not!

Do I need private health insurance to get ambulance cover?

In some states, yes you do. It all depends where you live. The government website summarises it well in the table below:

State	Ambulance Cover arrangements in your state of residence
All states and territories	Department of Veterans Affairs Gold Card holders are covered for state ambulance services in every state by the Department.
ACT	Health Care Concession Card and Pensioner Concession Card holders are entitled to free emergency ambulance services. If you are not eligible for a concession and want to be covered, you can purchase insurance from a private health fund.

State	Ambulance Cover arrangements in your state of residence
NSW	Health Care Concession Card, Pensioner Concession Card, and Commonwealth Seniors Health Card holders are entitled to free ambulance transport services. If you are not eligible for a concession and want to be covered, you can purchase insurance from a private health fund.
NT	Pensioner Concession Card and Commonwealth Seniors Health Card holders are entitled to free ambulance transport services. If you are not eligible for a concession and want to be covered, you can purchase insurance from a private health fund or a subscription through the state ambulance service.
Qld	Ambulance costs for Queensland residents are covered by the state government.
SA	If you want ambulance cover you can purchase insurance from a private health fund or a subscription through the state ambulance service.
Tas	Ambulance costs for Tasmanian residents are covered by the state government.

State	Ambulance Cover arrangements in your state of residence
Vic	Pensioner Concession Card and Healthcare Card holders are entitled to free ambulance transport services. If you are not eligible for a concession and want to be covered, you can purchase insurance from a private health fund or a subscription through the state ambulance service.
WA	Aged Pensioner concession holders are entitled to free ambulance transport services. If you are not eligible for a concession and want to be covered, you can purchase insurance from a private health fund or a subscription through the state ambulance service.

Source: www.privatehealth.gov.au/

What if I've got a pre-existing condition?

Pre-existing conditions stop a lot of people from switching or taking up health insurance because they assume they can't. The truth is, pre-existing conditions *do* make it more complex, but it's not impossible. Here's what the ombudsman says: 'a health insurer may impose a 12-month waiting period on benefits for hospital treatment for pre-existing conditions . . . Once a member has been on their hospital policy for a continuous period of

12 months, the pre-existing condition waiting period no longer applies and the member is entitled to the full benefits under their policy.' (NB: If you've served this waiting period with one insurer, you don't have to serve it again with another, if you switch to 'comparable cover'. Just be upfront and ask the fund you want to move to whether there's any extra waiting periods and you should be fine.)

What level of cover do I need?

Only you can answer this one, unfortunately. Think of it this way: insurance is a bet. It requires you to decide how much risk you can live with. Some of us are Evel Knievel and we love risk so much we're probably uninsurable! Others just can't sleep at night unless they're covered for any and all risks, and those people will just have to pay top dollar if they want a bit of shut-eye. You need to consider your own health and weigh up what's likely to go wrong, if anything. Then consider how much risk you're prepared to live with.

Then pick a policy to fit you (or *no* policy if that's more appropriate).

The cheaper policies have lots of 'exclusions'. That's why they're cheap. There's nothing wrong with that, as long as you know what you're getting for your money, so make sure you know what you're trading away when you downgrade your policy.

Collect your Green Belt, Grasshopper

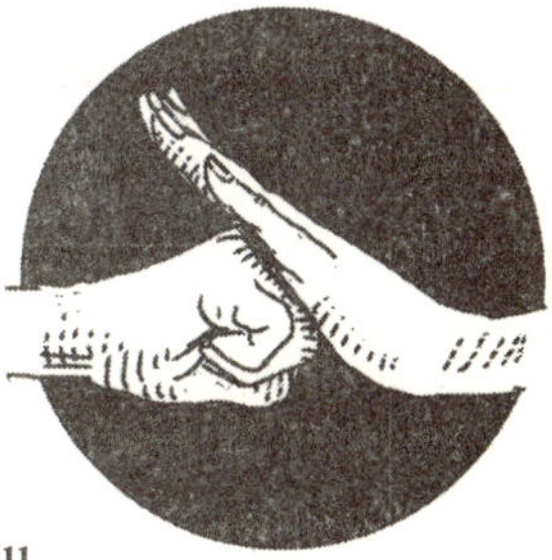

If you've read every chapter up to this point, you deserve some sort of award!

I wish I could buy you a drink or present you with a plaque, but you'll have to settle for another Bill-Killing Belt. A Green one this time.

You're starting to look dangerous. Your bills are quaking in their envelopes every time you walk past.

So keep it up because you're on a roll. Next up we tackle credit cards.

CHAPTER 14
CREDIT CARDS

If you love your plastic and you take out special deal after special deal to rack up points and move your balance around, please accept my apologies. You won't like this chapter much.

I used to do that too until my uber-sensible other half pointed out to me that it made no sense. Like a lot of people, I was paying 20% interest on my credit card debt and I had savings earning a fraction of that in another account.

The hard truth, which I learnt myself the hard way, is that the best way to save on credit cards is to pay them off and chop them up.

If you want to know how they talk about you behind closed doors at your credit card company and you're interested in weaning yourself off the plastic, read on.

You can just try the 'Quick Bill-Kill' approach below, or you can hone your plastic-chopping skills by reading the entire chapter - up to you.

But if you're not prepared to take your medicine yet and replace your credit card with a debit card (they're the ones where you actually spend money you really *have*), you might want to skip to Chapter 15, where we discuss petrol.

At a glance

Potential saving	$700 a year by switching, or many thousands by paying it off
Degree of difficulty	1 out of 5
Best times to save	Anytime
Time required to switch	From 10 minutes
Top online tools	Commercial comparison sites such as finder.com.au, canstar.com.au, creditcardcompare.com.au
If I could tell you one thing about credit cards it would be:	You probably don't need them. And most of us are better off without them if we don't pay them off every month.

QUICK BILL-KILL: Credit Cards

The best way to save on credit card bills is to pay them off. Simple as that. #sorrynotsorry

But sometimes it helps to minimise your interest rate while you do it. So, here's a four-step guide, but it *only* works if you use it to pay the balance down.

1. **Go to finder.com.au, canstar.com.au or creditcard-compare.com.au and search for 'Balance Transfer Cards'.** Look for a card with a long balance transfer period. In some cases, you can pay 0% interest for about two years on the balance you move from another card. Ideally, pick one that also has a low or *no* annual fee and a low or *no* 'balance transfer fee'.
2. **Divide your balance by the number of months the balance transfer will last (eg $3000 divided by 26 = $115.38).** You're going to set up a regular transfer from your monthly pay to cover the amount. (If there's no way you can cover it in that time frame, you have two choices: look at a 'low rate' credit card instead and pay it down over a longer period, or call the National Debt Help Hotline on 1800 007 007 or go to financialcounsellingaustralia.org.au and ask for their help.)
3. **Apply to move your credit card balance to the new balance transfer card.** Move any direct debits you have set up onto your new card. Close the old card. Chop it up!

4. **Now put the new card in a tray of water and pop it in the freezer, thereby encasing it in ice like Han Solo in *The Empire Strikes Back*.** You are going to try to never use this card. It'll be there for emergencies, but you'll have to wait for it to thaw while you take a good long hard look at yourself!

HARD TRUTH: You're either a 'Revolver' or a 'Transactor'

You know those people who like to say 'There are two types of people'?

Well, the people who work in the credit card industry are those people.

In their eyes, you're either a 'Revolver' or a 'Transactor'.

If you spend a small fortune on your credit card through your business (or your family) and you pay the balance off each month, then you might be amassing thousands of reward points and paying no interest, in which case you're a winner.

To credit card insiders, you're what's called a 'transactor', and frankly you're not much use to them.

But if, like most of us, you've constantly got a few grand on the card and you're always paying interest, you're what's called a 'Revolver', my friend. And you're their ideal customer.

KILLER STAT: In 2019, Aussies were paying interest on more than $30 billion of credit card balances, according to the RBA.

It might sound kinda sexy, but 'Revolvers' are the mugs of the credit card world. They're the reason banks and other lenders make billions from the not-so-fantastic plastic, and why Australians usually have an average credit card balance of about $3500.

True Story: I was a Revolver too, but now I'm a smug ex-Revolver!

They say it's always the ex-smokers who get in your ear most fervently about quitting the fags.

Well brace yourself, because credit cards can be the cancer sticks of the financial product world, and I'm a reformed addict.

Like most Australians, I applied for a credit card in my twenties, and then lived beyond my means for about 15 years. I only chopped it up at age 40, and only because I married someone more sensible than me and she eventually wore me down.

Don't get me wrong. I was never one of those people who rack up $10,000 or $20,000 on the plastic. I was just Joel Average. I had smack bang on the national average credit card debt of about $3500, and it never really changed. I'd pay it off with my tax refund, and a year later it'd be back to $3500.

But I was paying about $700 a year in interest that I really didn't need to, just for the privilege of being able to spend someone else's money.

I've now got a debit card that does everything the old credit card did, except spend someone else's money. Sometimes there's nothing left on it, so I stop spending until there's something on it again.

Sometimes I miss it. But I don't miss that feeling of being in debt. And neither will you. Unless you're a bona fide 'transactor' and you've mastered the art of maximising card rewards while paying no interest, I heartily recommend quitting.

(I know you 'Point Hacks' types are out there, but I also know most of us aren't frequent flyers and we're in denial about what the real costs of cards are.)

The best insider tricks to use on . . . credit cards

David's Slingshot

Good news! Credit cards are up there with telco products for the easiest bills to compare online. The internet really has made it a piece of cake to find a cheaper card.

In fact, some of the biggest comparison websites started out only doing credit cards because they were so easy to compare online (finder.com.au is now the most-visited comparison website in Australia, covering more than a dozen different household bills, but it started out as creditcardfinder.com.au).

This means you can find and apply for a cheaper card in the time it takes to drink a cup of tea or coffee, if you know what you're looking for.

You'll just need to decide first of all whether you're a 'Revolver' or a 'Transactor' (be honest with yourself), and therefore whether you need a low rate or balance transfer card (for Revolvers) or a rewards or gold or platinum card (strictly for Transactors).

INSIDE INFO: When you're on these websites, they will sometimes show you preferred partner offers first. Make sure you scroll down a bit and look at all the offers on the first page. Or check the box saying you want to see *all* results, not just their favourites.

The Elizabeth Taylor

In the 'Quick Bill-Kill' earlier, I explained how to make the most of a balance transfer offer to pay down your card. If you're cunning, you might have read that and thought 'I could just do that over and over again and enjoy interest honeymoon after interest honeymoon, Liz Taylor-style.'

And you'd be right. It is possible to go from balance transfer offer to balance transfer offer, and some people do.

There are pitfalls in this strategy, however: for one, it could leave your credit report looking like something the dog ate, and then brought back up, and then ate again.

Your credit report or credit score is often described as your financial CV: lenders use it when deciding whether to lend to you. So if you make a lot of applications for credit in a short period of time, it's there for anyone to see and they may count it against you when assessing an application.

According to finder.com.au, 'Each time you submit a credit card application, the credit card provider assesses your application by requesting a copy of your credit report. This is called a "hard credit inquiry" and is recorded on your report for up to two years, regardless of the outcome (which is not recorded). Hard inquiries aren't limited to credit card applications; you get one every time you apply for any kind of loan, mortgage or utility credit. Each hard inquiry can take a few points off your credit score. While occasional hard enquiries are unlikely to hurt your credit score, imagine having a bunch of them together on your report within a short period of time. To a lender, it could look as if you're desperate for credit, and definitely raises a red flag when they are assessing your application.'

The other danger in this strategy is that balance transfer offers often revert to a high rate at the end. They might seem enormously generous, but they're designed by data geeks who know from their research that most people won't pay the balance down and will then end up paying the full interest rate (often 20% p.a. or higher) after the honeymoon ends. And many people won't remember to apply for another balance transfer before the higher rate kicks in.

The Squeaky Wheel

Got a problem with your provider of plastic?

Remember the three-step guide from Part 1 on 'How to Whinge Well':

1. First: whinge (politely) to the boss (in this case, all providers of financial products have to have an internal dispute resolution process so you'll probably be directed to complete that form).
2. If that fails: whinge (politely) in public.
3. If that fails: whinge (politely) to the regulator.

For financial products, the regulator is AFCA, or the Australian Financial Complaints Authority. You can contact them on 1800 931 678 or head to their website: www.afca.org.au

AFCA can conciliate between you and the provider, they can ask for further information to help deal with your complaint, and they can make a decision that's binding on the provider, if it's accepted by you.

When it comes to credit cards, here are some of the long list of things AFCA deals with:

- Advice you received or that was not provided to you about a credit product that may have been inappropriate or misleading.
- Charges that were incorrectly applied, or costs that were calculated or charged incorrectly – such as break costs, fees or commissions.
- Disclosures that were incorrect, insufficient or misleading information about costs or fees, or about the product provided to you.
- Financial difficulty where your request to vary your repayments was declined or not responded to – or you've been issued a default notice.
- Decisions about irresponsible lending, or if you believe that a financial firm is pursuing you for a debt that is not yours or not outstanding.
- Instructions you gave that the financial firm did not follow or delayed in following.
- Privacy and confidentiality including complaints about consumer or commercial credit reporting, or where you were refused access to personal

information, and other privacy breaches including inappropriate collection or use (including disclosure) of personal information.

- Transactions such as incorrect or dishonoured transactions, mistaken payments or unauthorised transactions.

They can't consider complaints about the level of a fee, premium, charge, rebate or interest rate 'unless your complaint is about one of the issues outlined on this page'.

The Red Dog

There are websites devoted to getting the most out of credit card joining offers and reward schemes. The best-known of these is called 'Point Hacks', and it's legendary among points-chasers. There's also 'I Fly Flat' and others springing up by the day.

In fact there's a whole thriving subculture out there of people who play the credit card rewards game like it's high-stakes poker. These people have been reading this chapter and shouting at the book, 'No! You fool! This guy has no idea what he's on about!'

Like most gamblers, 'point hackers' like to tell you about their wins and some have been known to rack up enough points to fly First Class just by amassing special offers and exploiting various tricks and loopholes.

And good luck to them! They do exist. Some of them

are my closest friends. If you can pull it off, then more power to you.

But I've left it out of this book because strictly speaking, it's not a money-saving strategy per se. It's more a reward-maximisation strategy. It also involves spending quite a lot, albeit while ensuring you get maximum payback for your spend.

If this sounds like your bag, the place to start learning more is pointhacks.com.au, where self-taught Frequent Flyer Points guru Keith Mason has turned his years of experience into a business teaching others how to play the game too.

7 other ways to save on credit cards

1. **Pay the balance off every month:** Your card might say you get '55 days interest free on purchases', but here's the catch: if you don't pay it off each month, that interest holiday gets reversed, and you pay interest on all your purchases.

> **INSIDE INFO:** Pay off your balance each statement and you won't be charged interest. But if you don't pay it off, not only will you be charged interest on that balance, but you'll also lose the 'interest-free period' on any future purchases until your balance is zero.

2. **Apply for a super-low rate credit card:** There are plenty of credit cards with rates under 10% and low annual fees. They won't have all the bells and whistles of rewards cards, but check for yourself: how many rewards are you *really* getting for your high interest rate and big annual fee?

> **KILLER STAT:** One Qantas Frequent Flyer point is generally worth about 1–1.5 cents.

Using points to upgrade your existing flight bookings is one of the most effective ways to use your points, followed by booking flights and then redeeming for gift vouchers and products.

But don't be fooled: as a rule, you need a lot of points to buy products. In March 2019, RateCity looked at the worst big bank cards for redeeming products through the Qantas store and found that to get a $200 SMEG kettle, you needed to spend:

- $133,470 on ANZ Frequent Flyer
- $77,860 on Westpac's Altitude Qantas
- $74,520 on NAB Qantas Rewards
- $55,280 on NAB Rewards Classic
- $51,900 on Commbank Awards

3. **Never pay the 'minimum repayment' if you can afford to pay more:** The minimum repayment varies but it's normally around 3% of what

you owe. Pay that each month and it'll only take you about 60 LONG YEARS to be debt-free (and that's assuming you don't put more on the card). So you should always pay more than the minimum repayment. Pay the lot if you can.

4. **Don't take out cash advances:** When you take cash off your plastic, you pay interest (often about 20% per annum) from the day you do so, and you also pay a cash advance fee. Double whammy!
5. **Don't blindly accept whatever credit limit they offer you:** The bank will decide what limit they want to offer you. So what? Since when did they know what's best for you? Decide for yourself. What's the maximum you're prepared to owe them? Set that as your limit. They're no longer allowed to offer you increases without you asking for them – unless you give them permission to do so. If you don't want to be offered credit limit increases, tell them that's your preference.
6. **Consolidate your credit cards:** If you've got multiple cards with balances on them, why not move all that debt into one place with as low an interest rate as possible, and then pay it down? It could be a balance transfer card (if you think you can clear it during the balance transfer period) or a low rate card, or even a personal loan – which will remove the temptation to keep putting more debt on the new card.
7. **Cancel after 11 months:** If you're a 'transactor', you might be able to apply for a special deal with no

annual fee for the first year and cancel the card after 11 months. Some canny types use this loophole to access special joining offers that give you as much as 100,000 bonus points. But do bear in mind the warning above about taking too many 'honeymoons' when it comes to credit cards and loans: it can sometimes hurt your credit score.

Everything you wanted to know about credit cards (and then some . . .)

What's the average credit card balance?

It changes constantly, of course, and our debt levels are coming down a bit lately (Aussie, Aussie, Aussie!) but at its peak in 2017 ASIC's Moneysmart estimated that the average Australian had $4200 on the plastic, paying $700+ in interest per year at rates mostly of 15–20% p.a. That's about half the average electricity bill, but for some reason we don't often think of credit card costs in the same way as other household bills. We really should.

How do interest-free periods work?

Most credit cards offer up to 30, 44 or 55 days interest-free on purchases, but you don't get it in most cases if you don't clear your balance by the due date each month. Also, they usually advertise 'up to' because you might get the full number of interest-free days if you buy something at the start of the billing cycle, but

KILLER STAT: The corporate watchdog riffled through Australia's pockets in mid-2017 and found that, when it comes to credit cards:

- Australians had a combined balance of $45 billion on our cards.
- We were paying $445 million a year in interest & $1.5 billion in fees.
- About one in two Aussies had a card.
- One in three of those had more than one card.
- One in 20 even had more than five credit cards!

buy it at the end of the billing cycle and you get none if it's a 30-day interest-free card - or 14 or 25 days if it's a 44- or 55-day interest-free card.

What do I do if there's a dodgy charge on my credit card?

Call the card provider ASAP and report it. Get a reference number for your report so you can prove you acted quickly, because this can be key to minimising the damage.

Most card providers are signed up to a code that says they should return your money, according to ASIC, if:

- a forged, expired, faulty or cancelled PIN/password or card was used;
- the transaction was fraudulently made by an employee of your financial institution or merchant;

- the transaction took place before you received your card, PIN or password;
- a merchant incorrectly debited your account more than once;
- the transaction occurred after you told your financial institution that your card was lost or stolen, or that someone else may know your PIN or password;
- it's clear that you haven't contributed to the loss.

On the other hand, you might not get your money back if you acted fraudulently, didn't keep your PIN secure, delayed telling them for too long, or accidentally left your card in an ATM. But there are caps in the code on how much you can be liable for.

Which type of card is right for me?

We might aspire to being the jetsetter with a platinum credit card, gold frequent flyer status and a boarding pass for Seat 1A (all posted to Instagram with the hashtag #winning, of course). But if that really is you, you're probably reading the wrong book.

Most of us are down the back end of the plane (if we're even on it), among the screaming kids, the mouth-breathers and the banging toilet door. Because that's where all the real fun happens! And we should choose the card to match. The first step on the road to credit card savings is: *be realistic*.

Cards are like cars – you wouldn't buy a Porsche SUV if you can't afford the upfront cost, the fuel bill and the expensive European parts. So don't apply for the Porsche of credit cards if you're a Hyundai driver (like me! Nothing wrong with Hyundai drivers.)

Here's a rundown of the different types of card, who they're best for, and what type of car they'd be if you were buying one of those instead.

Are rewards schemes worth it?

This one is up there with 'What's the meaning of life?' and 'Why did God invent mosquitoes?' It's the $64,000 question when it comes to credit cards, and it's very hard to answer.

INSIDE INFO: After extensive research I've come to the conclusion that most rewards schemes are *designed* to be confusing. This is because the points are not worth much in real dollar value, so the goal of the points scheme architect is to make you believe they're worth *more than they really are*. There's a lot of talk about points and 'bonus points' and holidays and shopping on their websites, but not much about the actual, no-BS dollar value of their points. If you're not a big spender, and you're not into numbers, consider dumping the rewards card if it's costing you anything in the form of card fees or higher interest – and skipping the rest of this chapter.

CREDIT CARD	IF IT WAS A CAR . . .	GOOD FOR	PROS	CONS
Low rate cards	**Trusty five-year-old Toyota Corolla**	'Revolvers': People who are unable to repay their credit card debt in full at the end of each month – as the interest charged is minimal.	Simplicity and price; they often have an annual fee of $100 or less and rates can be less than 10% p.a.	No complimentary perks and benefits such as frequent flyer points, free insurance and access to airport lounges; but you can still sometimes get a balance transfer deal, giving you 6–24 months of 0% interest to pay your debt down.

CREDIT CARD	IF IT WAS A CAR . . .	GOOD FOR	PROS	CONS
Reward point cards	**New Mazda or Volkswagen**	'Transactors': People who spend a lot on their credit card and pay it off each month	Joining offers can feature up to 100,000 points, and you can earn points from all your everyday spending and bills.	Often have a higher annual fee and/or a reward programme fee, and a higher interest rate. Check the fees don't outweigh the rewards! It will come down to how much you spend on the card.

CREDIT CARD	IF IT WAS A CAR . . .	GOOD FOR	PROS	CONS
Balance transfer cards	**Silver Service Taxi**	'Revolvers' or 'Transactors': Anyone who wants to minimise credit card costs for a limited period of time.	People who want to consolidate debt and pay it down over a set period of time.	There is sometimes a fee of around 2% of your balance, and they usually revert to a high rate. Taking offer after offer can also hurt your credit score (see above).
Gold and platinum cards	**Porsche SUV**	Travelling 'Transactors': People who spend a lot, travel a lot and can afford the higher fees and interest rates.	Common benefits include bonus points, lounge passes at airports, and complimentary insurances such as purchase protection, travel insurance or car hire excess insurance.	A much higher annual fee (e.g. $500) and interest rate (e.g. up to 25% p.a.). Also, higher minimum credit limits (e.g. $15,000) so you need to be disciplined about keeping the balance down.

In fact, the answer is constantly changing because the value of a rewards point is constantly changing.

In mid-2018, the value of points was cut because of some new 'interchange fee' rules that the government brought in, so for many of us the answer to this question is now 'Yeah, nah, not really'.

Still here? Ok then, you asked for it ... Here goes nothing.

As a basic rule, you need to see what the cost of accessing the rewards scheme is, and compare that to the value of the rewards you get over a year.

If 'Cost of Rewards > Value of Rewards', it's not worth it, and vice versa.

The cost of access is the easy bit: it will usually be an annual fee on the card, and these can range up to $500.

There might also be a cost to join a rewards program such as Qantas Frequent Flyer if you're not already a member.

Another cost of access is the higher interest rate on rewards cards, averaging about 20% p.a. (Although if you pay the card off each month, you can ignore this one.)

As for the value of rewards, this is where it gets tricky. Working this out can make your brain ache. But here's one (relatively) simple way to do it:

1. Estimate your weekly spend on the card (look at a statement), then multiply that by 52 weeks to get your estimated annual spend.

2. Work out how many reward points you'll earn over the year. (e.g. Two points per dollar spent means you multiply the annual spend by two, and so on.)
3. Now that you know roughly how many points you'll earn in a year, you can go to the website of the relevant reward scheme and see how many gift cards your annual points balance would buy (I just checked mine and 55,000 points only gets me about $250 of gift cards, for example).
4. Or, you can use a 'points calculator' like the ones below to see what your annual points would buy you in frequent flyer points, and you can use the usual cost of those flights to estimate the value.

Point Hacks Points Calculator: www.pointhacks.com.au/community/tools-calculators/credit-card-reward-program-conversion-calculator/

Credit Card Compare Points Calculator: www.creditcardcompare.com.au/tools/calculators/rewards-calculator/

Are you *still* here? Ok, well this is where this chapter enters the Twilight Zone. If you make it to the end of the next part, pour yourself a tall glass of something nice because you'll have trekked right into the dark heart of the credit card rewards jungle and returned to tell the tale.

DID YOU KNOW: Two Beautiful Mind-type maths geniuses recently created an equation to predict the likelihood of losing socks in the wash. It's called the 'Socks Loss index' and it looks like this:

$$(L(p \times f) + C(t \times s)) - (P \times A)$$

What does that have to do with credit card rewards? Well, at financial comparison website Canstar.com.au, they have their own credit card rewards equivalent of the Socks Loss Index. Their in-house Beautiful Minds have created a mathematical equation to calculate whether you're better off with or without a particular rewards credit card. They call it 'Net Reward Return' and it looks like this:

$$\frac{\text{POINTS EARNED IN A YEAR}}{\text{POINTS REQUIRED TO REDEEM \$1 OF REWARD}} = \text{REWARD RETURN}$$

So let's say you spend $24,000 a year on your card and earn 24,000 points, and your rewards scheme requires 150 points to redeem $1 of value on a gift card or other reward.

Canstar reports that your equation will look something like this:

$$\frac{\$24\text{k} = 24{,}000 \text{ points}}{150 \text{ points} / \$1} = \$160$$

Because your 'Net Reward Return' comes out at $160, you'll be better off with this card if your annual fees and costs for having the card are *under* $160. You'll be worse off if they're over that amount.

Get it? I did warn you . . .

Collect your Blue Belt, Grasshopper

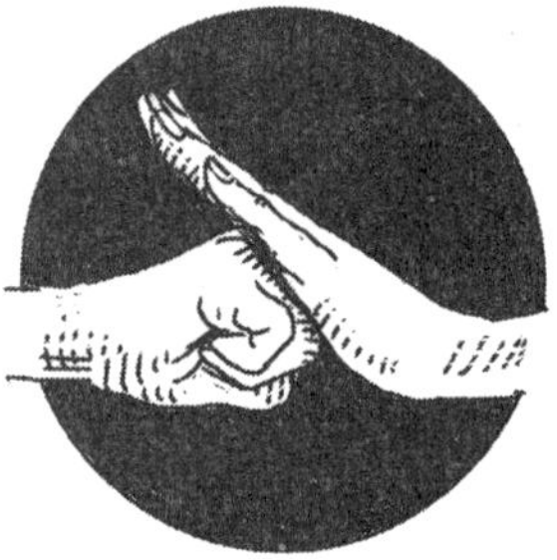

Well yippee-ki-yay! You're fast becoming the Bruce Willis of money-saving.

If Bill-Killing was a real martial art, you'd now be a Blue Belt.

Next up we'll tackle a couple of bills that are unavoidable but instead of being a big monthly or annual cost, they're weekly or even daily. It's time for petrol and groceries.

CHAPTER 15
PETROL

There aren't many bills that irritate Australians like petrol does.

In this chapter I'll explain why I think that is - what's unique about fuel and why it gets us so hot under the collar.

We're a nation of drivers so there's no avoiding our volatile petrol prices, but there are ways to minimise what you pay.

With some other bills, if you just get it right once a year, Robert's-your-father's-brother and you're set for 12 months. But not petrol.

Petrol is a daily or weekly challenge and killing this

bill is more about getting into the right habits, which can save you hundreds or thousands over time, depending on how much you drive.

Try the short 'Bill-Kill' savings guide below if you're in a hurry, or read on for all sorts of insider info on how petrol pricing works in Australia and how to stay on top of it.

At a glance

Potential saving	Up to $10 a tank (more for bigger cars)
Degree of difficulty	3 out of 5 (depending on where you live)
Best times to save	When the price cycle is at its lowest
Time required to save	A few minutes at a time
Top online tools	Motormouth app, Fuel Map Australia app, FuelCheck app (NSW), MyFuel app (NT), www.accc.gov.au/consumers/petrol-diesel-lpg/petrol-price-cycles
If I could tell you one thing about Petrol it would be:	Use one of the new apps. Technology is your petrol-price-saving friend.

QUICK BILL-KILL: Petrol

If you don't have the time or energy to go the whole hog on minimising your petrol bill, but you're still desperate to save a few hundred bucks each year, there are two golden rules to making a saving on fuel bills: fill up at the right place, and fill up at the right time.

1. **Fill up at the right place:** Don't just go to your nearest petrol station every time. Save up to 20 cents per litre by using a smartphone app to check the cheapest petrol in your area. If you don't have much of a range to choose from, pick one loyalty scheme that suits you and stick to it – Coles, Woolies/Caltex, 7-Eleven all have them and many motoring clubs have four cents per litre discounts with certain retailers such as Caltex and Puma.
2. **Fill up at the right time:** Don't wait until the fuel light comes on. Save up to 20c a litre by always filling up on a day when petrol is cheap. You can check which days are best by using one of the new fuel apps or checking the ACCC 'petrol price cycle' website: www.accc.gov.au/consumers/petrol-diesel-lpg/petrol-price-cycles

PS – Sharing is caring! Post your petrol savings and tips to @OneBigSwitchAU and @KillBillsBook with the hashtag #KillBills and we'll share them with all the other Bill-Killers out there.

HARD TRUTH: Petrol prices are finally emerging from the dark ages

Imagine every single electricity retailer or mobile network provider advertised their prices on large signs as high as a house along the side of every major road, so you couldn't miss them even if you tried. And imagine they then changed those prices every day - sometimes more than once in a day - and they also charged different amounts from one suburb to the next. And imagine also that the only place you could find those prices was on those signs, by driving all the way to that part of town to check them.

Crazy, right? Well, that's how petrol used to work in Australia.

And that's why it's so different to our other household bills. Everyone knows what it costs, whether they want to or not, and everyone can see that the prices are all over the shop. But they've always been very, very hard to compare without a lot of driving . . . until now.

The internet catches up with everyone sooner or later, and the petrol industry is finally getting a taste of what it's like to be dragged kicking and screaming into the 21st century.

Not every state in Australia has created an app where petrol retailers have to post their prices so that you can compare them all without driving around looking at the signs. But some have, and we hope it's only a matter of time until they all do.

Meantime, the new smartphone apps ask drivers

to post prices so they can give 'crowd-sourced' information.

Even the old shopper docket loyalty schemes (while not as generous as they used to be) are finally heading online. Soon it'll be no more carrying the paper dockets around and digging through your purse or wallet at the counter to try and locate one that hasn't expired!

Technology really is your friend when it comes to winning this war. And instead of one big battle a year that could save you hundreds, it's lots of small skirmishes where little savings add up over time. So you'll need to use the tricks below on a weekly basis, and be patient.

Good luck.

A word from the consumer watchdog

A 2019 report from the ACCC revealed how motorists can save 15–20 cents per litre by avoiding buying petrol at the peak of the price cycle.

The analysis of the Australian petroleum industry showed that there were six days in the preceding six months when petrol prices were at their peak - and the ACCC says if motorists didn't buy E10 fuel on those peak price days they could have saved an average 2.6 cents per litre, using Sydney as an example.

'Motorists who fill up weekly can make substantial savings by avoiding the six most expensive days in the price cycle,' ACCC Chairman Rod Sims said. 'Motorists that can fill up less frequently, however, and therefore buy petrol when prices are falling can save much more.

'For example, avoiding buying petrol on the 10 days around the price cycle peaks would see motorists save 3.8-6.1 c/l in the capital cities. This would see annual savings of $141 million in Sydney, $124 million in Melbourne, $68 million in Brisbane and $55 million in Adelaide.

'Our advice for those looking to save even more, say 15-20 c/l, or $9-12 a tank, is to time your purchases.

'Use fuel price transparency apps or websites to find the most competitive fuel price near you. There can be significant price differences between sites at different points in the price cycle, so motorists that shop around can save themselves a lot of money.'

Hear, hear.

The best insider tricks to use on . . . petrol

David's Slingshot

Remember: the key to killing petrol bills is filling up at the right place, at the right time.

It used to be almost impossible to know where the cheapest petrol was at any time (at least without burning a lot of petrol driving around looking at the signs!), but technology is finally breaking down the barriers to comparing prices.

If you're in NSW and the NT, you're lucky - your state government has forced petrol stations to report their prices several times a day to a government fuel app.

In WA, you're also lucky - your state government has created Fuelwatch, which locks in each price for 24 hours and makes your petrol cycle more predictable (usually fill up on Mondays, if you can).

In other states, there are slightly less sophisticated apps that have been created by private businesses that can still help you to find cheap fuel - usually by combining publicly available data with updates from app users.

Here are some of the current apps to try, and some info about their strengths and weaknesses. Best of all, they're mostly *free*.

FuelCheck NSW & MyFuel NT apps

Best for: NSW & NT

Where to get them: App Store, Google Play.

- Offers the choice of 11 different fuel types across all brands.
- Provides up-to-the-minute information and data as well as fuel price history.
- Predicts price trends and suggests the best days to fill up.
- Covers both metro and regional areas.
- Only offered in NSW and NT at present.

FuelWatch website/email service (WA)

Best for: WA

Where to get it: fuelwatch.wa.gov.au

- Offers the choice of six different fuel types across all brands.

- Provides daily prices for 600 plus retailers and fuel price history.
- Predicts price trends and suggests the best days to fill up.
- Covers metro and most regional areas.
- Only offered in WA at present.
- Does not offer a mobile app yet.

Motormouth app

Best for: outside NSW, NT & WA

Where to get it: App Store, Google Play.

- The most comprehensive 'national' app for petrol prices. Claims to report prices for around 4500 Australian service stations each day.
- Covers both metro and (some) regional areas.
- Predicts price trends and suggests the best days to fill up.
- You have to click on a station to see the price: it doesn't automatically display them. And after checking 30 prices in a week, you have to 'top up' for free (for some strange reason).
- Outside NSW and NT, it relies on participating service stations and users to report prices, so the data is 'crowd-sourced' and patchy. Some stations only report a 'range'.

MyNRMA app (NSW only)

Best for: NRMA members

Where to get it: App Store, Google Play.

- Offers the same features as the FuelCheck and MotorMouth apps in NSW, but also includes an NRMA member discount of up to five cents per litre with participating Caltex petrol stations.
- Only available if you're an NRMA member (but you can now pay just $5 a month for 'NRMA Blue' membership).

RACQ Fair Fuel Price app (Qld only)

Best for: RACQ members

Where to get it: App Store, Google Play.

- Offers many of the same features as the MotorMouth app in Qld, but also includes a RACQ member discount of up to four cents per litre with participating Puma petrol stations.
- Also nominates a 'fair price' for petrol in your area each day, so you'll know which stations are having a lend of you.
- Only available if you're a member, but you can join the 'Lifestyle' package for just $26 a year.

RACV app (Vic)

Best for: RACV members

Where to get it: App Store, Google Play.

- Offers many of the same features as the MotorMouth app in Vic.

- Also nominates a 'Don't pay above' price for petrol in your area each day, so you'll know which stations are having a lend of you.
- Only available if you're an RACV member (but you can get a 'Personal Membership' for $36 a year).

TIGHTARSE TIP: The RACV fuel price map is actually available for free on their website if you really want to use it for nix! Go to www.racv.com.au/on-the-road/driving-maintenance/fuel-prices.html

The Red Dog

The 'De Niro' Trick I described in Part 1 applies to petrol as much as it does to any other bill. Being fiercely disloyal and being prepared to walk away whenever you see a better deal is the key to paying as little as possible for your fuel.

But petrol is also one of those rare bills where there are, in fact, rewards for being loyal.

Loyalty schemes won't always deliver you the cheapest price – if you want to pay bottom dollar, you'll still need to compare the independents and use the new pricing apps to see who's cheapest on the day.

But if you do pick a loyalty scheme and stick with it,

you will save hundreds on your petrol bill compared to someone who just pulls into the next servo each time the fuel light comes on.

You might only have a Coles and a Woolworths fuel outlet nearby, for example, and in that case it pays to pick and stick with one. Or you might do all your shopping at Coles, and have your insurance and credit card with them too - in which case it might make sense for you to buy their fuel.

So here's a rundown of the fuel loyalty schemes that exist. Note that they're constantly changing, but I've done my best to report the latest versions at the time of print.

There's no 'best' scheme in my view - picking a winner will usually depend on other factors such as where you do your grocery shopping, or which stations are on your commute, or whether you already belong to a motoring club that offers a discount.

Just pick one that works for you and make the most of it.

Woolworths & Caltex

Customers who spend at least $30 at the supermarket earn a discount on fuel. Your supermarket receipts contain a fuel discount offer on the back that is redeemable at all applicable service stations within Australia - and if you have a rewards card, it is also stored on the card for 28 days.

Woolies says there are 520 plus Caltex Woolworths fuel outlets available for discount holders to pick from.

What's more, there are 100 plus additional Caltex redemption sites.

You earn one Woolworths Rewards point for every dollar you spend at participating outlets.

You can also redeem your four cents per litre fuel discount at any of these locations, and combine it with another four cents per litre offer for spending $5 in-store at the petrol station, making an eight cent per litre discount overall. (But note that not *all* Caltex servos accept the Woolies vouchers.)

One difference between Woolies and Coles is that the Woolworths fuel app now allows you to get your discount without keeping the paper receipt.

Coles & Shell

Like Woolies, customers who spend at least $30 at a Coles supermarket earn a discount on fuel. Your supermarket receipts contain a fuel discount offer on the back that is redeemable at all applicable service stations within Australia.

Coles says there are nearly 700 Coles Express stores around Australia. With Flybuys you can also earn points on fuel: one point for every $2 spent.

Meanwhile, if you spend $20 at any participating Coles Express store, you can save 10 cents per litre on fuel. Add that to your Coles Supermarket four-cent fuel discount docket and you can save 14 cents per litre on fuel.

You do need to keep the paper dockets, though – Coles has still not moved into the digital age on this one.

Coles & Woolies Gift Cards

This is another way to save 5% on fuel. You can often get a discount of 5% off Coles and Woolworths Gift Cards, some of which can be used to buy petrol. To find these deals, you can look at money-saving websites such as Groupon and Ozbargain and The Entertainment Book, or if you're a customer of the following they often have them as part of their own rewards programs: RACQ, NRMA, RACV, RAA, RAC, AGL Rewards, Suncorp Benefits, Employment Hero, Skoolbag Family Essentials.

TIGHTARSE TIP: Hardcore money-savers use these cards to pay at both the supermarket and the petrol station and combine them with the four cents per litre shopper docket discount and other in-store offers to maximise their savings.

For example:

- Buy a Wish Gift Card with $100 credit for $95 (a 5% discount).
- Pay for your shopping with the gift card.
- Take your fuel discount to a Woolworths Caltex petrol station.
- Pay for your petrol with the Gift Card and the shopper docket discount.
- Get an extra four cents per litre off for spending $5 in-store at the petrol station.
- Drive away smugly, basking in the knowledge your petrol was cheap as chips.

7-Eleven/Mobil

At 7-Eleven/Mobil they have a fuel app that allows you to lock in a cheap price for seven days if you have one of their fuel cards and you pre-load it. They call it 'fuel price lock'.

In the early days of the app, some cunning motorists found a loophole where you could turn off your phone's GPS, lie about where you were, and lock in a price from anywhere in the country for a week. By now 7-Eleven/Mobil seems to have caught on to this trick and addressed it in later updates of the app, so this cheap fuel party might be over for the time being.

Motoring Clubs

Motoring Clubs such as the RAC in WA and the RACQ in Queensland have a four cents per litre discount with Puma petrol stations. You need to be a member, which costs money, but if you're already a member it's worth checking out.

The Moving Target

The biggest challenge with finding cheap petrol has always been the volatility of fuel prices. They 'rise like a rocket and drop like a feather', so filling up a day late can cost you $20 or more per tank.

But fill up at the right time, every week, and depending on the size of your car and how much you drive, you could save anywhere from $250 to thousands of dollars a year.

While price cycles *used* to follow a rough weekly pattern, they don't anymore (except in WA, where it's *almost always* cheapest on Monday and rockets upwards on Tuesday).

In other states it used to be 'Cheap Tuesdays' were the best day of the week to fill up, but they're now a thing of the past.

These days, you've got to find out where the cycle is up to in other ways - and once again the key is technology.

Most of the apps mentioned above will show you a graph of average petrol prices in your area and give you a recommendation of which days to fill up, so that's one way to check.

If you don't use apps, you can get the same info on the ACCC website, updated three times a week, at this link:

www.accc.gov.au/consumers/petrol-diesel-lpg/petrol-price-cycles

(or just Google 'ACCC petrol price cycle').

In regional areas, you'll find it a lot harder, unfortunately - neither the apps nor the consumer watchdog covers price cycles in regional Australia.

9 Other ways to save on petrol

1. **Go indie:** Independent petrol stations are usually cheaper than the majors, often by about four cents per litre (which is exactly the value of the shopper

docket schemes run by the big supermarkets, co-incidentally ... or maybe not coincidentally at all). If you're disciplined about using the supermarket dockets, you'll probably spend about the same as if you buy at independents.

2. **Buy your petrol at Costco:** This one only works if you have a Costco membership (about $60 a year) and you're near a Costco warehouse that sells fuel (there are only 11 nationwide, all in the major east and south-eastern cities). But if that's you, Costco fuel is cheap as.

INSIDE INFO: Costco usually has the cheapest petrol in Australia. As I write this, the cheapest E10 Unleaded in Sydney today is 121.7 cents per litre at Costco in Casula. That's 15 cents per litre cheaper than the Sydney-wide average and it's a whopping 38 cents per litre cheaper than the top price of 159.9 cents per litre across town at Malcolm Turnbull's local servo – the BP in Edgecliff!

3. **Cut back on driving time:** It's obvious but it needs to be said: fewer kilometres clocked up means more fuel in the tank. Also, a cold engine uses more fuel as it warms up, my revhead mates tell me. So take a bus

from time to time or ride a bike for short trips, and try to combine your daily errands into one longer journey to really maximise your fuel efficiency.

4. **Avoid peak hour:** This is pretty much the secret to everlasting happiness in life, if you ask me. But peak hour is also the worst time to drive for fuel efficiency. You're constantly stopping and starting, braking and accelerating, shifting up and down between the gears, and that sucks up the juice. Your car is most fuel-efficient when it's humming along the motorway at 110 km/h. So do more humming along and less kangaroo-hopping, and you'll save on fuel.
5. **Try carpooling:** Another obvious one, but if you've got a neighbour who's heading the same way as you, or a workmate who lives nearby and isn't the world's worst company, why not take turns driving and halve your weekday fuel bill? One of you can also get some personal admin done on your phone in the meantime, or call into radio stations to complain about the traffic and young people these days.
6. **Downsize:** Smaller car = smaller engine = smaller petrol bill. Finance guru Paul Clitheroe famously says you should 'buy the cheapest car your ego can live with' - because cars depreciate so badly. Bigger cars also cost more to run, as a general rule. So if you don't have a SUV-sized ego and you're not ferrying 2.5 kids and their associated piles of stuff around, why pay for a SUV-sized car?

7. **Go easy on the air con:** It's funny how we get used to creature comforts. My first car was a 1984 Peugeot 505 with no air con and I used to take it up the coast on long summer roadtrips in 35-degree heat. No problemo! These days I couldn't survive in a car in summer without AC, but it does use extra petrol so go easy on it if you can.
8. **Pump your tyres up:** Inflate your tyres to the maximum recommended pressure (they should have a recommended range written on the side of the tyre somewhere). This can improve fuel consumption by up to 2%, and it also makes your tyres last longer.
9. **Go electric:** Electricity ain't super-cheap either, of course, but electric cars do cost less to fuel than petrol cars. The cars themselves cost more at present, so you'll need to factor that in, but it's only a matter of time before the prices come down.

Petrol cars cost about 3–4 times as much to run as electric cars. The folks at My Electric Car estimate that it costs approximately $4.50 in electricity to travel 100 km in an electric car. 'In comparison, the average petrol car in Australia uses 11.1 litres of fuel to travel 100 km. (Australian Bureau of Statistics). That's a cost of $16.65 to travel 100 km at $1.50 per litre. Even a very efficient diesel vehicle (5 litres per 100 km) will cost $7.50.'

The Qld government is a bit more conservative but they still say that if you drive 13,300 km a year, an electric car will cost about $1000 less to fuel.

Everything you wanted to know about petrol (and then some . . .)

Why is petrol so expensive in Australia?

Tell that to a Kiwi and they'll laugh at you. Aussie petrol is cheap as, bro! They pay about 50 cents per litre more than we do. Our fuel prices are high, but we're somewhere in the middle by international standards. The graph on the next page from the industry lobby group shows how good we have it.

I think we get all wound up about petrol prices because we're a nation of commuters and we drive a lot, and because they go up and down so much that we feel like someone somewhere overseas is having a lend of us.

Obviously we don't have oil reserves in Australia, so it has to come from overseas and that leaves us at the mercy of international wholesale prices and the value of the Aussie dollar.

KILLER STAT: Average fuel prices have almost doubled since 2002 when they were around 87 cents per litre, according to the Australian Institute of Petroleum.

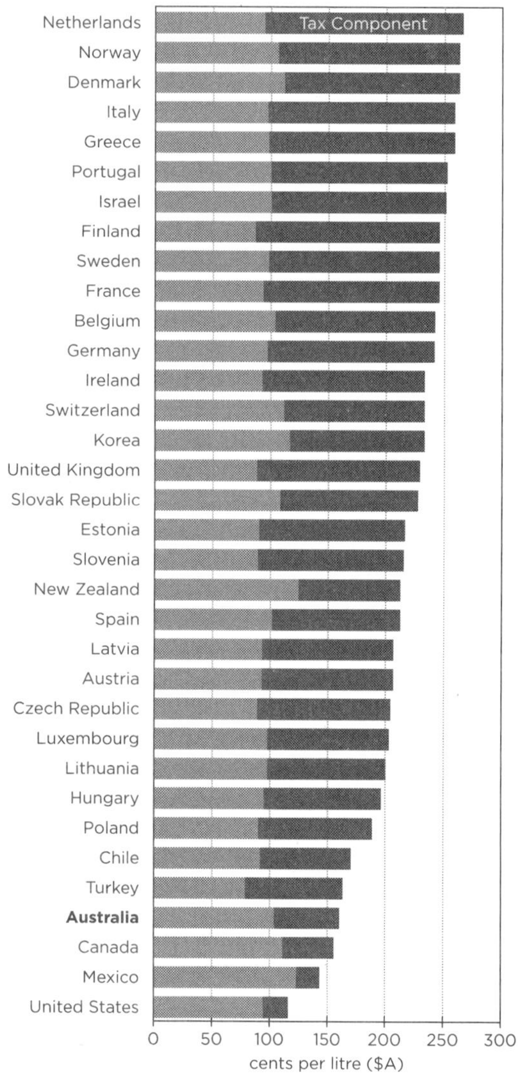

Source: Australian Petroleum Statistics, Office of the Chief Economist.

Whatever happened to Cheap Tuesdays?

It used to be that the petrol price cycle in eastern cities was predictable, and you could usually just fill up on Tuesdays to save. But now the cycle is as long as about five weeks (except in Perth! Fill up on Mondays in Perth!).

The cycles are now less predictable, but because they're slower you've got a bit more time to fill up when the prices start to rocket upwards. You've also got a new weapon in your armoury: smartphone apps. Look around for a servo that hasn't raised their prices yet and go for it.

Is petrol more expensive on public holidays?

It often seems like it is, but the consumer watchdog says this one is a furphy. 'Our last detailed review of prices in the five largest cities around every public holiday found that, on average, public holiday price increases were no larger than the usual price cycle increases during the year. These price rises may be more noticeable before holiday weekends because many motorists are making long trips and using more petrol than usual.'

Why do petrol prices fluctuate so much?

Pump prices at your local servo are influenced by the Singapore wholesale price of petrol (otherwise known as the Singapore Mogas 95 Unleaded Price, to your average petroleum industry geek), plus taxes and importing costs.

But the numbers on the signs are also shaped by old-fashioned supply and demand in each region. And finally there's a bit of lightweight corporate espionage that goes on, where retailers watch each other's prices and adjust theirs accordingly.

More competition in bigger cities usually means greater choice and lower prices for the consumer, however in small towns with fewer retailers, you'll pay about seven cents more.

Below is a graph from the ACCC showing how our prices sort of follow the international benchmark price, but not always . . .

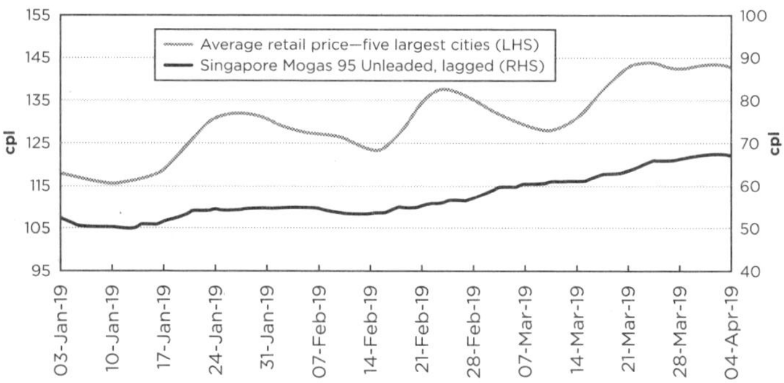

Source: Australian Competition and Consumer Commission, FUELtrac, OPIS and Reserve Bank of Australia

Which state has the most expensive petrol?

Queenslanders, you're not imagining it! Brisbane usually has the priciest petrol out of the five major capitals, according to the ACCC. Perth occasionally topples Brisvegas from its pedestal, though, as it did at the end of 2018, when Perth prices were 1.5c/l higher than Brisbane on average.

Does petrol cost more in the bush?

It sure does, and not just in the bush proper. Anywhere outside metro Australia, the price goes up. In 2018, the annual average difference between regional prices and those in the five largest cities was 6.9 cents per litre.

You're now a Purple Belt, Grasshopper

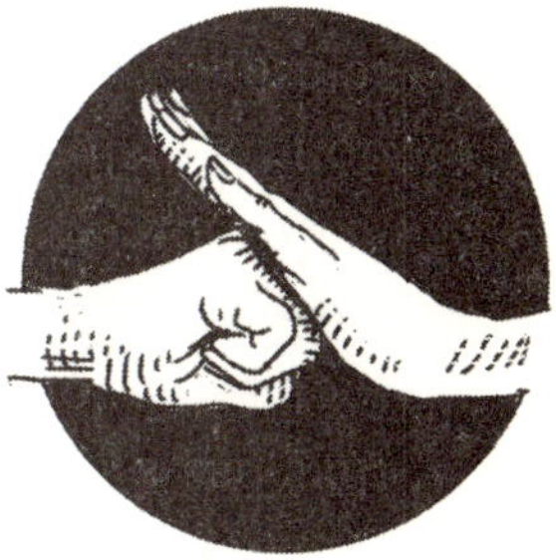

If you're reading this book from start to finish, you get a new Bill-Killing Belt with each chapter you ace.

So you're now a Purple Belt, and Black is just around the corner.

First, though, we've got to tackle that other big daily or weekly bill - the groceries.

As Tony Barber might say, let's go shopping . . .

CHAPTER 16
GROCERIES

To kill some bills - home or car insurance, for example, or energy - you just need to win one annual battle and you can wave to the crowd and sing the national anthem because you're the champion for another year or so.

Groceries ain't like that, unfortunately. They're a bit more like petrol in that sense: to really kill this bill, you need to win several small skirmishes every week.

I won't lie - I almost left groceries out of this book, because this book is about showing you how easy it can be to save hundreds or even over a thousand bucks in an afternoon if you're determined not to be ripped off and you've got the right inside info.

But by now you're a money-saving grown-up, so you can take it. If you've read the earlier chapters in this book, you're now a Purple Belt in the art of bill-killing karate, and you've made it this far, so I'm prepared to level with you.

The war on groceries is a war of attrition. It's more Western Front than Operation Desert Storm, more three-hour Oliver Stone movie than one-hour Michael Bay blockbuster.

You'll get a $2 saving here, and a $50 saving there. And over time it all adds up to thousands of dollars back in your pocket. But it's fiddly. As with petrol, you need to decide how much time and effort you've got for this one and just give it what you can.

This chapter is about getting into certain habits that will ensure you avoid paying top dollar for your groceries every time you hit the supermarket.

And in the long term, if you're determined to spend less on your household bills, these habits will be worth getting into – because for most of us groceries are the second-biggest household bill of them all, behind only the mortgage or rent.

At a glance

Potential saving	Anywhere from $1000–$5000 a year, depending on how determined you are

Degree of difficulty	3 out of 5, because it's a week-in, week-out tussle, not an annual one-off battle
Best times to save	Every week of the year
Top online tools	Half Price app, Shopfully app, Supermarket apps
If I could tell you one thing about Groceries it would be:	Shop at two supermarkets if you can: Aldi, and one other.

QUICK BILL-KILL: Groceries

Stuck for time but still determined to save a few bucks on the weekly grocery shop? Here's a list of the basics I think we should all be across:

1. **Make a list:** It seems obvious, but saving on groceries starts with good planning, and good planning starts with a list. Once you have a list, you can . . .
2. **Check out the weekly specials on a Wednesday:** Smartphone apps and websites such as 'Half Price' and 'Shopfully' now allow you to quickly scan the weekly specials at two or three supermarkets and see which of them are on your list. Make a note on your list so you know where to buy those items.

3. **Pick a shopping centre with multiple supermarkets, and go to Aldi first.** There is stiffer price competition at these shopping centres, and research shows the best way to save on groceries is to do at least some of your shopping at Aldi. So go to Aldi first and buy your basics, plus whatever specials you have marked on your list from step 2 above.

TIGHTARSE TIP: Do *not* buy anything from Aldi's notorious 'middle aisle'. I know those ski pants and footbaths and ugg boots can look irresistible, but this is where your Aldi savings strategy can quickly turn into an Aldi budget blowout!

4. **Shop at one other supermarket:** Coles and Woolies have very similar pricing, so which one you choose is up to you. But visit a second supermarket to get those items Aldi doesn't have, plus your weekly specials. Again, avoid impulse buys and do *not* fall for the displays on the ends of the aisles. It's a Tim Tam trap!

Share your Savings! Post your Grocery wins or tips to @OneBigSwitchAU and @KillBillsBook with the hashtag #KillBills and we'll share it with all the other Bill-Killers out there.

HARD TRUTH: From Little Savings, Big Savings Grow (with apologies to Kev Carmody and Paul Kelly)

'From little things, big things grow,' as the song goes.

That could be a motto for the supermarket business.

Add up every can of baked beans and every banana and every litre of milk sold, and all up, supermarkets in Australia earn more than $100 billion a year, reports IBIS World. That's very big bikkies.

They do that by making a tiny bit out of you on each item, because at the end of your shop it adds up to a substantial margin for them.

And their goal, from the moment you walk through the door, is to increase your 'basket size' and maximise the number of high-margin items in it.

But the Kev Carmody–Paul Kelly classic is also a good song to sing to ourselves as we wander the aisles at the supermarket. Our goal needs to be the equal and opposite of the supermarkets: save a tiny bit on each item, and achieve lots of tiny savings that amount to one significant saving over time.

For most of us, this is our second biggest bill. You do your weekly shop and you only buy 50 or 100 different items that all cost not much, but they add up to an average of $240, according to the ABS's Household Expenditure Survey. That's $12,000 a year.

Big bills mean big potential savings, even if it's the sum of lots of little wins. Find a way to reduce the cost of every item by 20%, for example, and there's a potential saving on offer of over $2500 a year for that average household.

The insider tricks and other ideas below are about achieving lots of little wins in the battle against big grocery bills, which will add up to thousands over time. But in the end, the number of wins you can collect will be a function of how much time you have to devote to the task - and when it comes to groceries, everyone just has to do the best they can with the time they've got.

A few ways supermarkets entice you to spend more

Supermarkets have a pricing strategy that uses certain specials as 'bait' to get you in the door and then certain other products as their margin-makers.

The $1 milk at the back of the shop? Probably one of the most successful baiting strategies ever invented, even if it has squeezed some dairy producers to near-bankruptcy . . .

The weekly specials? Also designed to get you in the door, even if they sometimes make a loss on those items.

On the other hand, the Tim Tams and fresh raspberries lovingly presented on the end of the aisle so you must walk past them to get to the cheap milk? That's often where they make their moolah, and it's also where your bill can blow out.

So you'll need to be aware of the tactics they use to make you spend more:

The layout: the shop is designed to maximise the time you spend there and 'cross-sell' you high-margin items that probably weren't on your list. IKEA is the worst example of this - it makes you follow a single, meandering path through every section if you want to get out of the place, but supermarkets do a bit of this too. The milk is up the back. The expensive health foods are often on the way from the entrance to the milk. The cheapest products are on the higher and lower shelves with the more expensive ones at eye level. Look up! Look down! Close your eyes as you walk past the Tim Tams.

The checkout: from magazines to chewie, chocolate and batteries, they use the checkout to suggest to you a final couple of small purchases while you wait in line. Ker-ching! They also use them to entice the kids to pester you to buy stuff that's no good for them. Resist!

Smells and sounds: The best exponents of this one are those Danish ice-cream shops that pump out the waffle cone smell to entice you in. Gets me every time. But supermarkets do a bit of this too sometimes, pumping out the smell of baking bread and using music to make you comfortable and keep you wandering the aisles for longer.

End-of-aisle displays: these are highly visible spots that they can sell to a particular brand or use to push a high-margin product. It's not the best place to buy your Tim Tams. If Tim Tams are on your list, at least go to the biscuit section where you can see what's on the high and low shelves, use the unit pricing and grab any specials that week.

The best insider tricks to use on . . . groceries

The De Niro

If you've just opened the book at this chapter, you'll need to understand that the 'De Niro' is named after a role the great American actor played in the 90s and it's all about being prepared to walk away at any moment. And it really does pay to be heartless when it comes to your grocery bill.

It's universally acknowledged by all the experts that the best way to pay as little as possible for your groceries is to shop at two or even three supermarkets and pick the eyes out of their specials and their specialties.

If things are really tight and you've got the time and the determination to maximise your savings, this is the way to go.

But it's quite a big job, isn't it? I'll admit that I get to two shops at the most when I do the weekly grocery run, and sometimes just one – so if you're like me you'll probably get more out of reading the other insider tricks below.

Still here? Right. You are very dedicated, Grasshopper, and more power to you.

So here's what you have to do to play the supermarkets off at their own game.

Find out what's on special at your local supermarkets each week, add that to your list, if you need it, and buy it first, avoiding the high-margin products where possible.

The best way to check the specials before you hit the road is by using a Grocery-saving app that scans multiple catalogues, or by using the supermarkets' websites or apps yourself: start with the 'half-price specials' as these are usually the biggest discounts.

Grocery Saving apps (See 'David's Slingshot' below)

- Half Price (on the App store or Google Play): Scans the catalogues to let you know what's 50% off, so you can stock up on things you need when they're cheap or plan your list around them.
- Shopfully (on the App store or Google Play): Collects all the catalogues in one place so you can look at them before you hit the shops.

Coles

- Download the 'Coles' app on the App store or Google Play.
- Or subscribe to email catalogues: www.coles.com.au/catalogues-and-specials/register-for-catalogues
- Or check the website: www.coles.com.au/catalogues-and-specials/view-all-available-catalogues

Woolworths

- Download the 'Woolworths' app on the App store or Google Play.
- Or check the website catalogue: www.woolworths.com.au/shop/catalogue

Aldi

- Download the 'Aldi Australia' app on the App store or Google Play.
- Or check the website for 'Super Savers' specials: www.aldi.com.au/en/groceries/super-savers/

Once you've done your weekly sleuthing and made your list, go to two or even three supermarkets to hunt down the specials, preferably at a shopping centre where they're co-located (I'll explain why below).

Also, do a trip to Costco every quarter if you live near one, to stock up on non-perishables and fill your petrol tank while you're there. (Costco has Australia's cheapest petrol, but it's for members only.)

When you go to Costco, go with someone else so that you can buy some really big bulk items and share them, and while you're at it, why not share a membership, which costs about $60 a year - you'll make that back if you make a few trips each year.

Another bulk-buying strategy is to join or create a fortnightly fruit and veg syndicate and take turns to go to the markets on a weekend and get everyone's fruit and veg in one fell swoop.

INSIDE INFO: There's another reason why the multiple-supermarket trick works too: good, ol'-fashioned competition. Coles says that 'store managers ... have the discretion to lower prices on individual items to compete in local markets, which means prices sometimes vary slightly on individual items between stores'. Translation: some prices may be lower in shopping centres that have multiple supermarkets.

So ideally you won't just shop at two or three supermarkets, you'll *also* do it at a shopping centre where all three are co-located, like seagulls fighting to the death over every hot chip. (That's you. You're the hot chip.)

The Mystery-Shopper

Usually this trick is about going undercover to see if a retailer is treating you right. But in this case, relax ... someone's already done the legwork for you.

In 2015 and 2017, consumer group CHOICE sent their undercover mystery shoppers into 110 supermarkets – 32 Coles, 32 Woolworths, 26 Aldi and 20 IGA stores – in 33 locations across Australia.

They bought the same basket of 33 common items (including beef mince, chicken, Nutri-Grain, OMO, Tim Tams, Coca-Cola, Dairy Farmers Milk and five fresh fruit and vegetables, if all available) and then they compared the cost of the basket at each supermarket and averaged them out.

The finding, both times they did it? Aldi's cheaper.

There's not a great deal of difference between Coles and Woolworths pricing, probably because they monitor each other so closely.

But if you're prepared to forgo the name brands at Coles and Woolies (at least in 2017), CHOICE found you'd save an average of:

- 49–50% on Aldi's home brand products;
- Up to 59% on Aldi's budget products.

Even when you look at like-for-like comparisons, Aldi was:

- about 10% cheaper than Coles and Woolies for home brand products, on average;
- 6–8% cheaper than Coles and Woolies for budget brand products, on average.

(Remember how the average household spends $240 a week, or $12,480 a year, on groceries? Well, a 10% saving adds up to $1248 over the year.)

Now, Aldi ain't for everyone. Some people swear by it; they love the dairy and the meat and the weird middle aisle that features everything from ski gear to onesies.

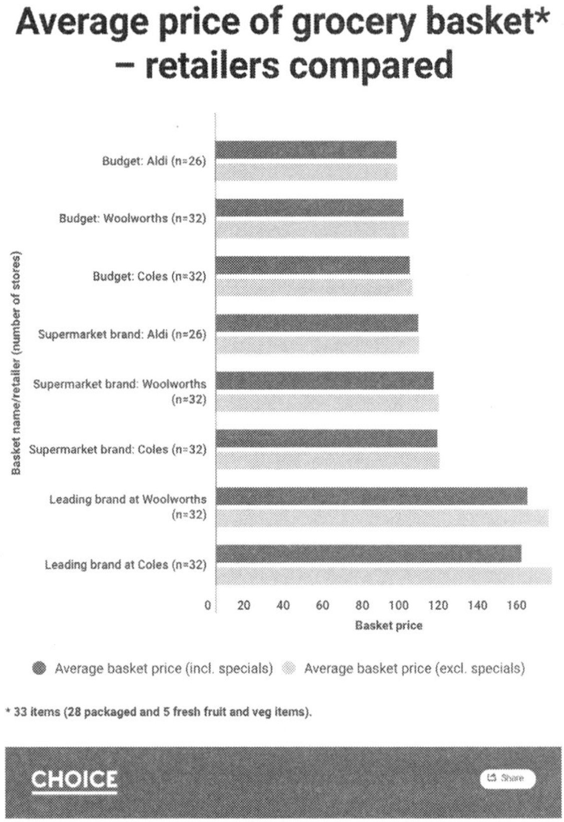

But some people say they just can't get their heads around it; they love their big brands too much, or they hate packing their own groceries (one way Aldi keeps its prices down), or they just don't have an Aldi nearby.

At last count, the German raider had about 500 stores across the country and was spreading from the east coast to SA and WA. You can see if there's a store near you or one opening soon on their website.

In mid-2018, they became the most trusted brand in Australia, according to researcher Roy Morgan's Net Trust Score. So they're the real deal, and German competitor Kaufland is on its way here next.

Aldi for Beginners

If you decide that Aldi is part of your grocery bill-killing armoury, here are some basics you'll need to get your head around:

Super savers

These are Aldi's weekly specials, and they're super-cheap. They post them on their website each week, or you can check them in the newsletter and the app (subscribe on their website). They're also marked in-store.

Copy cats or phantom brands

It's a very grey area when it comes to copyright and intellectual property, but Aldi's main strategy is to make their own cheaper products that look and taste as similar as possible to well-known brands. They've been called 'copy cats' and 'phantom brands' because they often look suspiciously like the originals, but the Aldi products are usually cheaper. About 90% of Aldi products fit this bill, but they also stock a handful of big-name products too.

Award-winners

Certain Aldi ranges such as their dairy and alcohol are highly-rated by Aldi shoppers and have won independent awards. Their cheeses, for example, picked up 49 medals at the Sydney Royal Cheese and Dairy Show in 2013 and their Blackstone Paddock Margaret River Cabernet Sauvignon 2015 wine ($17.99 a bottle) won Gold at the prestigious Royal Adelaide Wine Awards.

Special buys

Aldi's famous twice-weekly 'Special Buys' each Wednesday and Saturday feature discount items in their 'middle aisle' such as furniture and electrical goods. There's a theme each week (one week: ski gear, next week: garden tools) and most Aldi shoppers have a story about going out for some milk and coming home with a footbath! My tip for the middle aisle is to avoid it altogether, unless you *really* need something they're offering that week. Sign up for the newsletter and/or the app, check that week's special buys before you go shopping, and if you don't *need* any of them, avoid avoid avoid. The notorious middle aisle is the Bermuda Triangle of supermarket money-saving expeditions. Many a frugal shopper has walked by, glanced sideways at some 100% merino under-garments and never. Been. Seen. Again.

You can subscribe to Aldi's e-newsletter or download their apps on the website at aldi.com.au.

The Red Dog

If you don't have the time (or frankly, you can't be bothered) shopping at more than one supermarket, fair enough.

But you can still be smart about your weekly Coles or Woolies shop. How much you save on groceries depends entirely on how much time you're able to put into saving. If you're time-poor, there is a Plan B: pick a winner and stick to them like you-know-what to a blanket.

The Red Dog is a calculated tactic whereby you show kelpie-like levels of loyalty to a provider because they make it worth your while.

There are different reasons to pick and stick with each of the three biggest supermarket chains. Which one works for you will come down to your circumstances, really - which ones are nearby, where you buy your petrol, whether you prefer lowest prices or maximum rewards.

I've laid out the case for Aldi pretty clearly above. If you want to pay bottom dollar for groceries, I think you've got to at least buy your basics from Aldi, if not most of your groceries.

But it's not an option for everyone, and some of us have other reasons to pick one of the big two supermarket chains. Here's the case for each of the big guys so you can make your own call.

The case for Coles: convenience, rewards, petrol, financial products, price

Coles is about the same price as Woolies but cheaper than IGA, according to the CHOICE mystery-shopping experiment described above.

But the #1 reason to pick and stick with Coles is convenience: they're just about everywhere.

Most people will pick a supermarket not too far from home: after all, there's no point burning $50 of petrol driving across town to save $49 on your shop.

And Coles has over 800 of them all over Australia.

Coles also has its Flybuys rewards program, which is how they reward you for picking and sticking - the more you sign over your financial life to them, the more rewards love they give you.

Here's how Coles rewards you for loading up on their products:

- **Petrol:** Spend $30 or more at Coles and you get a petrol voucher that gives you four cents per litre discount at almost 700 participating Coles Express stations. There are also fuel discounts for spending in-store at Coles Express so you can increase your discount to 14 cents per litre sometimes.
- **Flybuys:** You get a Flybuys point for every dollar you spend at Coles (and also at a range of other Flybuys partners, which may be a selling point for you). When you reach 2000 points, they'll offer you $10 off your next shop when you're at the Coles cashier. You need a lot of Flybuys points to redeem

them for anything meaningful but if you go all in on Coles products you can earn up to six points per dollar and collect them much quicker. For example, use a Coles rewards credit card with one of their many Flybuys partners and you'll earn two points per dollar spent.

- **Financial Products:** The more of these you have, the more points you earn with each dollar spent at Coles. In the most extreme example, if you use a Coles rewards credit card to pay for your shop, plus you have a Coles Home Insurance policy and a Coles Landlord Insurance policy and a Coles Car Insurance policy, you could end up earning six Flybuys points for every dollar you spend at Coles.

(These schemes are really confusing, but if you're a glutton for punishment you can read all about how it works on the Coles website: financialservices.coles.com.au/flybuys-fasttrack)

Case for Woolies: convenience, rewards, petrol, financial products, price

It's gobsmacking how similar Coles and Woolies are, really, when you look at all that they offer.

Woolies' pricing is also cheaper than IGA and about the same as Coles, albeit more expensive than Aldi – according to that same 2017 CHOICE research.

And the #1 reason to pick and stick with Woolies is also convenience: in fact, they claim to have even more stores than Coles, with about 900 around the country.

If you decide to go all in on Woolies, their rewards program also gives you a point for every dollar you spend at their associated group stores.

But there are some tiny differences with how their rewards cards work and how they reward you for taking out their credit cards and insurances. Details are below.

Here's how Woolies rewards you for loading up on their products:

- **Petrol:** Spend $30 or more at Woolies supermarkets and you get a petrol voucher that gives you four cents per litre discount at over 520 participating Caltex Woolworths fuel outlets, or 100 plus additional Caltex redemption sites. You can usually bundle this with an extra discount in-store at the petrol station to save even more so ask them what the latest offer is. Unlike Coles, Woolies also stores these on your rewards card so you don't need to dig out the paper receipt at the petrol station.
- **Woolworths Rewards:** You'll get a Woolworths Rewards point for every dollar you spend at Woolies, Big W, BWS or Caltex Woolworths fuel outlets (this range is smaller than Flybuys and Coles offers). Just like Coles, once you've got 2000 points, you can claim $10 off your shopping at the cashier. Woolies allows you to convert your points to Qantas Frequent Flyer points, whereas Coles has a deal with Virgin's Velocity Frequent Flyer program.

- **Financial Products:** With Woolies, you also earn extra points for using a Woolies credit card in-store. But they also have promos such as '10% off your shop once a month' if you use the card. Unlike Coles, you don't get extra rewards points for being a Woolies insurance customer, so there's a slight difference in approach. But on the whole, they're very hard to split!

If you're not confused enough already, there's more here: www.woolworthsrewards.com.au/how-it-works.html

David's Slingshot

Technology has been surprisingly slow to help us win the war on grocery bills. There's been wave after wave of new apps claiming to help you save but I find most of them are just glorified shopping list apps and seem pretty limited. Others arrive with much fanfare and then disappear soon afterwards.

I think two of the best at the time of writing are 'Half Price' and 'Shopfully'. A lot of apps help you manage your shopping list but these ones take the crucial extra step of scanning the weekly catalogues and (in the case of Half Price) telling you what the week's cheap specials are.

Half Price

- 4.7 stars, 500 plus ratings;
- free app;

- scans the Coles and Woolies catalogues and zeroes in on anything that is half price;
- Liquorland and BWS specials included too.

Shopfully

- 4.1 stars, 900 plus ratings;
- free app;
- like a 'catalogue of catalogues'. Scans most groceries (and other) catalogues so you can see them all in one place.

Woolies and Coles have spent up big on their own apps, which you should make the most of – either to check specials or to save your shopping list.

If you decide to go the full 'Red Dog' with either Coles or Woolies (see above), you can save your list on the app so you don't need to start from scratch each week and it will tell you when your regular purchases are on special.

But remember: these apps are designed to try to draw you into their orbit and make you commit to the exception of all others, amen. The best way to save on groceries is to flirt with multiple providers and use these tools like Tinder – the millennial dating app that lets you shop around for a different kind of 'special' entirely.

11 other ways to save on groceries

1. **Plan, plan, plan:** Make a list. Check it twice. Planning is key to saving on groceries because the enemy of supermarket savings is the dreaded

'impulse buy'. Start by checking what you already have in your pantry and fridge and writing a concise list of what you need to buy. This will help you to avoid 'browsing' or wandering aimlessly around the aisles buying double choc-dipped, caramel-filled Tim Tams, which is how a $200 shop can easily become a $250 shop.

2. **Declare a war on waste:** Make a rough meal plan for the week, and try to use up what you have for starters. Play 'surprise chef' with the contents of the back of your cupboard and it could save you as much as $1000 a year, which is the amount each household wastes on average according to the NSW government's 'Food Waste Avoidance Benchmark Study' in 2016.
3. **Never shop when hungry:** The hungrier you are, the more likely you are to . . . you guessed it: impulse buy. Approximately 57% of all Tim Tam purchases are made by hungry supermarket shoppers. (I made that up – I don't actually know that for sure. It's just based on, ahem, extensive first-hand research.)
4. **Don't shop with kids (if possible):** My kids, Master Seven and Miss Nine, surprised me recently by saying they *liked* doing the shopping. Are you serious, I asked? 'It means we get to beg for treats,' they said. Little buggers!

   It confirmed for me why I never take them to the supermarket if I can avoid it. I know that some of you never really have a choice, and you have

my utmost sympathy. I always smile at the people with kids in the supermarket. They must wonder what I'm mugging at. But shopping with kids can be a cruel form of torture. It takes you longer, you get ground down by 'pester power', and you can't properly concentrate on money-saving strategies such as the following . . .

5. **Use 'unit pricing':** Consumer groups fought hard to make grocery retailers say on their price tags what the cost of almost every product is per 100 grams. So make the most of it. This way you can take two different products in different-sized packets (or two packets of the *same* product in different sizes) and see how the prices *really* compare.

   Standard units: Most grocery items use a standard unit of measurement from the list below.

Type of item	Unit of measurement
Supplied by weight	per 100 grams
Supplied by volume	per 100 millilitres
Supplied by length	per metre
Supplied by area	per square metre
Supplied by number	per item included

Other units: Some grocery items use different units. For example, fruits and vegetables (per kilogram or per item), meat, seafood and poultry (per kilogram or per item) and drinks (per litre).

So look for the product that has the lowest unit price and opt for that – provided you're not buying such big portions that it'll go to waste, of course.

6. **Ever tried shopping at night?** There are a few reasons for the theory that it's cheaper to shop on, say, a Wednesday night than a Sunday morning. First, if you do it after dinner, you won't be hungry (see #3 above).

   Second, there are often end-of-day specials and price reductions as supermarkets try to get rid of stock – especially baked goods, fresh produce and other perishables.

   And third, crowds – or the lack of them. A more relaxed supermarket might be a better environment for a well-planned shop without impulse buys. Or so the theory goes. (Me? I'm usually too busy watching Netflix with a beer or vino after dinner. But each to their own.)

7. **Don't over-buy fruit and veg:** As I said above, we waste an average of $1000 per household per year and the #1 thing we throw out is fruit and veg. It's hard to plan for this one, but at least be aware of this when you decide how many bananas or kohlrabis to buy. (Tip: two kohlrabis is probably two too many.)
8. **Avoid packaging where you can:** It costs money to put stuff in packets and that cost will end up factored into the price. As a general rule, you'll pay less for unpackaged items (although do check the unit pricing in any case).
9. **Shop weekly, not daily:** There's always going to be those mid-week trips to restock bread and milk and whatever, but if you do your big shop once a week for non-perishables and meat, you'll minimise the number of impulse buys.
10. **Look up! Look down!** Like a lot of other shops, supermarkets put the high-margin products at eye-level where you're most likely to see them. They even charge those manufacturers extra for eye-level shelving or end-of-aisle displays. Chances are, the stuff with the lowest unit pricing will be on the top shelves or the bottom shelves.
11. **Don't shop online:** Online shopping is hugely convenient. It's also profitable for the supermarkets so they're really pushing us to do it. But if you want

to maximise savings, I think it's not ideal. There are a few reasons why: First, in the supermarket you can look up and down on the shelves and compare unit prices at a glance, whereas on the app or website that's harder. Second, you'll pay delivery charges. And third, bricks and mortar shops are often cheaper. As I said above, prices differ from shopping centre to shopping centre based on the level of competition. Online, you don't get the benefit of that. According to a 2016 'mystery shop' by Fairfax Media, buying groceries online can attract a 10% premium on the same products.

Here's your Brown Belt, Grasshopper

Now that you've shown those grocery bills who's boss, you've earnt yourself a Brown Belt in Bill-Killing.

Just two chapters left to go now and you'll be a fully-fledged Black Belt kung-fu master of money-saving.

A warning: the next chapter is about life insurance. But don't skip it - as you'll see, I've come up with a sneaky way of making it more fun than it sounds.

CHAPTER 17
LIFE INSURANCE

This will be the funniest chapter in this book, I promise. It'll also be the only chapter where I encourage some people to spend more.

This bill is like eating spinach, or like the annual prostate check or pap smear that we're told to have as we get older: It's not most people's idea of fun, but it is good for you and the people you love!

So ... This won't hurt a bit, and it will only take a minute or two.

It's important you read this chapter because chances are you don't have enough life insurance and you could be paying too much for whatever you do have.

As usual, there's a quick 'Bill-Kill' guide for those who just want a saving in as little time as possible, or read on to learn the skills you'll need to win this battle over and over again.

If you don't have life insurance or you have some but you know nothing about it, be sure to read 'Everything You Wanted to Know about Life Insurance' later in the chapter. Maybe even start there.

Oh, and one other thing. To reward anyone who *does* read this chapter, I've hidden six hilaaaarious dad jokes in it.

Skip these pages and you might not only go to your grave underinsured, but also dangerously under-amused.

At a glance

Example saving	$600 a year for a 60-year-old with $500,000 of cover
Degree of difficulty	3 out of 5
Best times to save	Anytime – but easier to switch while you're younger and healthier
Time required to switch	Starting from 30 minutes
Top online tools	Moneysmart.gov.au, Canstar.com.au, and your super fund website
If I could tell you one thing about life insurance it would be:	Many of us have some life insurance in our super, but most of us don't have enough, and much of it is overpriced.

QUICK BILL-KILL: Life Insurance

An Irishman walks into a chemist and asks for some deodorant. 'The ball or the aerosol?' asks the chemist. 'No, the armpit,' says the Irishman. While you think about that one, here's a five-step plan to hopefully getting more life insurance for less:

1. **First, work out how much cover you really need.** Do *not* use calculators on life insurers' websites, which have a curious tendency to over-inflate the number . . . Use the ASIC Moneysmart life insurance calculator at this link: www.moneysmart.gov.au/tools-and-resources/calculators-and-apps/life-insurance-calculator
2. **Second, check how much cover you have right now (in your super, and/or elsewhere).**
3. **Ask your super fund how much it would cost to increase your cover to the amount you need.**
4. **Get a quote also on a highly rated 'direct' life insurance policy for the extra cover you need.** At the time of going to print, examples of this type of cover were available from NobleOak and Allianz (check Canstar's ratings for the most up-to-date five-star policies).
5. **Pick a winner and go for it.** Or, if you have a financial adviser, show them the options and see if they can beat them! It's up to you.

We love to hear about your wins! Post your savings to @OneBigSwitchAU and @KillBillsBook with the hashtag #KillBills and we'll share it with all the other Bill-Killers out there.

HARD TRUTH: You're probably paying too much for not enough life insurance

There are almost as many life insurance policies in Australia as there are people, thanks to our compulsory superannuation system. Most super funds have automatic insurance included. But how many of us know if we're getting good value for our money?

The three things I think everyone should know about life insurance are these:

1. Most of us have some cover, but chances are it's not enough to cover our needs.
2. A lot of it has traditionally been overpriced.
3. And it might be dull or unpleasant, but imagine what it will mean to your family if something does

KILLER STAT: A staggering one in four of us have no idea if we even HAVE life insurance attached to our super, according to data from the Association of Superannuation Funds of Australia.

go horribly pear-shaped. Many policies will also pay out if you're diagnosed with a terminal illness.

And now, a word from the actuaries . . .

Actuaries are people who spend their days calculating the chances of things going wrong so that businesses can plan ahead – they're a bit like gamblers who bet on the losing horse instead of the winner.

Actuaries are not the life of the party. But they do have an irritating habit of being right, and they say that when it comes to life insurance, Australians are woefully underinsured.

According to Rice Warner, some of Australia's best-known actuarial experts on life insurance: 'For those who have life cover, the median cover level is estimated to be approximately $143,500, which is only twice the median household income.'

That might be ok if you die at 60, because Rice Warner reckons your family would need 1.6 years of family income to meet their basic needs if that happened (heaven forbid).

But die at 50, and they'll need 3.2 years of income, and kick the bucket at age 40 and they'll need 5.4 years of income just to get by.

Meanwhile, 30-year-old parents with kids, they say, should have:

- 8 times family income for life insurance;
- 4 times family income for TPD (total and permanent disability) insurance; and

- 85% of family income for income protection insurance.

That might sound like a lot of cover for a 30-year-old, but keep in mind these policies are cheaper when you're young. (A 30-year-old can get $500,000 of fully underwritten life cover for under $300 p.a. for a man and under $200 p.a. for a woman.)

Anyway, you get the idea. If most of us died or were too sick to work, our families would be up the creek with a paddle-pop stick. (By the way, what do you call a zoo with just one dog? A shih tzu.)

Exposed! The financial advice industry's life insurance gravy train

Until recently, financial advisers who sold you a life insurance policy were sometimes getting paid a finder's fee equal to your entire first year's premium by the life insurer!

That's why I say that a lot of life insurance has been overpriced. You don't need to be an actuary to see how that would have inflated premiums.

This cosy little rort has been cut back in the past couple of years, with a new 'shrinking' cap on commissions of 80% for policies started in 2018, 70% in 2019 and 60% from 2020.

As commissions come down, smaller amounts will hopefully be priced into the premiums, and there should be savings to be had.

This isn't a bill you can switch in five minutes, like electricity or gas. For the good products you'll need to answer a bunch of questions about your health and lifestyle so they can decide what to charge you. But the savings can be big, and the cost of not having enough cover can be even bigger for the people you love . . .

True Story: Vickie saves $1000s on a Saturday arvo by shopping around for life, trauma and income protection cover

Vickie from Sydney's inner western suburbs needed to save some money to move house and she had a nagging feeling she was paying too much for her insurances. She was right.

She switched her life insurance policy and downgraded her trauma and income protection policies, and saved 'thousands'.

'It was seamless. I got a call on a Saturday afternoon. A wonderful consultant spoke to me for over an hour. We worked through all the questions they needed to ask, and by the end of the day she'd sent me the documents I needed to sign. I signed them, sent them back and that was the switch. Simple.

'That was it. We switched and we'd saved thousands of dollars in one day.

'I've already recommended to a lot of people to investigate especially their life insurance because I think that's where you get to make the most gains.

'I had no idea how you could save so much, I thought it was fairly standard and clearly it's not.'

The best insider tricks to use on . . . life insurance

David's Slingshot

Ok, so most of us are underinsured. But how do we work out exactly how much cover we should have?

That's been a very difficult question to answer in the past. Most of the people willing to help you with it have been selling life insurance, funnily enough, and they made more money if you took out more cover (Oh, really! You say I need how much? Ten times my annual income?! That sounds like an awful lot, but, well, if you say so . . .)

But the financial services regulator has come to the rescue. ASIC's Moneysmart website has created a more commonsense calculator to tell you how much you need. Just punch your answers in at this link and 'Robert's your father's brother':

www.moneysmart.gov.au/tools-and-resources/calculators-and-apps/life-insurance-calculator

That reminds me of a joke. How many Spaniards does it take to change a lightbulb? Juan.

The De Niro

If you've done everything in this book up to this point, you've got some serious money-saving chops by now and you know exactly what this trick is all about – flagrant disloyalty!

When it comes to blind loyalty and bills, life insurance might just be the worst of the bunch.

I say that because most life insurance policies are picked for us by a super fund, an adviser or a planner, which makes us less likely to know if we're getting good bang for our buck.

In fact, I'll be a monkey's uncle if most people can even name their life insurance company off the top of their head. (Speaking of animals, what do you call a cow with no legs? Ground beef.)

But life insurance is also one of the best bills to go hunting for a big saving, because of the fat that's built into a lot of premiums and because the premiums can get very steep in later life.

The financial advice and planning industries will not like this book, because it encourages people to wade into the quicksand of financial products and try to make their own way out.

Fair enough. If you've got a broker or adviser or planner, you *should* take their advice on which life insurance policy is the right one. They ought to know their stuff.

But you should also know that in most cases they're paid for referring you to a policy, and that you can sometimes save a packet by cutting out the middleman.

Why not get an alternative quote yourself and show it to your adviser/planner/broker and see if they can beat it. That way you know that you're getting the best result – whether that's through them or 'DIY'.

There are three main places to go looking for cheaper life insurance yourself:

1. You can ask your super fund for a quote to *increase* the cover currently in your super account. This is often well-priced because the super fund 'bulk-buys' it.
2. You can bypass the middleman and go straight to one of the new breed of 'direct life insurers' that sell fully underwritten policies without going through an adviser or planner.
3. Or you can try one of the life insurance comparison websites. (Just make sure you're comparing like-for-like: if your policy is fully underwritten, for example, compare it to another fully underwritten policy.)

You can then compare the alternative quote to what you're paying now, and if you're not getting good value for money, you can switch or put your current provider on the spot.

Here's a basic script for what you'll need to say:

'Hi, my name is _______ and I've been a customer for ______ years. I've just noticed I pay $______ for $______ of life insurance cover and there are other providers out there offering $______ of cover for $______, such as [insert name of competitor you've got a quote from]. So I'm planning on switching. But I just thought I'd make one final call to see if you can give me a better deal than the one I'm on. What's the best deal you can offer me to stay?'

True Story: Queensland entrepreneur Joanne saves $1000 p.a. on two life covers

This is Joanne Kennard from Brisbane. She's a keen camper and an ideas person. Her inventions include the 'Easy Oven', a slow cooker made of fabric, and the 'Bush Barbie', a highly-efficient wood camp stove.

All-up, she runs about five different start-ups and small businesses from home. So she knows a bit about managing budgets. But even Joanne was surprised at how much the price of life insurance can differ from one provider to the next.

'Years of loyalty doesn't mean anything,' she told me recently.

With their old life insurer, Joanne and her husband's life cover cost them $5823.72 per annum.

When they shopped around and got a quote from a direct life insurer offering fully underwritten cover, they were quoted $4464.24 per annum.

That's almost $1400 less. And they also got 'two months free' for joining, which means they saved over $2000 in the first year. #BillKilled!

The Good Listener

Let's say you want to get a quote from a 'direct' life insurer to compare to the policy your super fund or your financial adviser has sold you.

How do you sort the good from the bad? It's an important question because direct life insurance policies are not all equal - some are pretty basic.

Fortunately, there are now a range of annual awards and star ratings for direct life insurance products that you can use to help sift the crap from the cream of the crop.

Financial comparison website Canstar has one of the best-known systems for rating these products.

Their experts assess each policy for 20 different types of customer across all ages, genders and smoker/non-smoker status. Then they apply a star rating for value based on its price competitiveness first (this makes up 70% of the rating), and features second (30% of the rating).

Their five-star products 'are the top 10% of products in their field', according to Canstar.

If it gets four stars, it has 'a good mix of price and features and shouldn't be struck off your shopping list, especially if the product and brand really appeal to you'.

You can check the latest results at their website but in 2018 the winners for direct Life insurance were:

- NobleOak;
- Allianz;
- Insure Me Now.

(Full disclosure: I have a NobleOak policy and we work with them to create special deals for our members at One Big Switch. We do that because NobleOak is a bit different to other direct life insurers, in that they offer the sort of fully featured, fully underwritten cover that you normally get via an adviser, but they sell it direct to customers and often at a substantial discount from so-called 'advised' policies. Check it out if you like the sound of that. And if you're not getting financial advice, remember to read the PDS for yourself. But you should be able to get a quote on any of the four- or five-star rated policies on Canstar and have some confidence you're not buying a lemon.)

True Story: Adam cuts his premiums by 10–12%

'I think my life insurance was a set and forget one. For at least 15–20 years I didn't really look at it.

'But I'm now saving between 10 and 12 per cent on my annual premiums, and I can tell you that makes me feel pretty happy.

'Switching life insurance takes a little bit of time because there's a lot of questions and answers to

go through . . . what you need in your cover and any pre-existing conditions you may have. That took a bit of time. But other than that it was really easy. The company did all the prep-work, sent through the documents, you check it and sign it and away you go.

'I say have a look at what you're paying. Don't just set and forget. Insurance companies love this, they just want you to roll over – but that's the worst thing you can do. You have to go back and you have to test the market. It's your money, you work hard for it, don't waste it.'

The Squeaky Wheel

Having a barney with your life insurer? As always, see if you can resolve any problems first by speaking to a manager and/or by having a public whinge to your life insurer (see the three-step guide to having a successful whinge in Part 1 of the book).

Then use the official channels if your problem doesn't get resolved easily.

Remember the golden rule of complaining: be polite and maintain your sense of humour. What happened to the refrigerator saleswoman? Kelvinator.

All financial product providers must have an internal dispute resolution process and, if that doesn't work, they're subject to regulation by the Australian Financial Complaints Authority, AFCA.

Since 2018, all new financial services complaints are dealt with by these guys. You can contact them on 1800 931 678 or visit their website: www.afca.org.au

AFCA can conciliate between you and the provider, they can ask for further information to help deal with your complaint, and they can make a decision that's binding on the provider, if it's accepted by you.

(But do note: ASIC says if you're complaining about a life insurance policy in your super, complain to your super fund first, not the insurance provider.)

Everything you wanted to know about life insurance (and then some . . .)

What's the difference between life, TPD, trauma and income protection insurance?

All these variations can sometimes be grouped under the general term 'life insurance' or 'risk insurance', but they're all slightly different:

- **Life cover**, aka term life insurance, aka death cover, pays a set amount of money when you die to the beneficiaries on your policy.
- **Total and permanent disability (TPD) cover** is often sold with life cover. It pays a lump sum if you are totally and permanently disabled. Note that some policies only cover you if you cannot undertake any occupation. The better ones cover you if you can't do your *own* occupation.
- **Trauma cover** pays out if you are diagnosed with certain illnesses such as cancer or a stroke.
- **Income protection cover** pays out if you can't work for a while because of injury or illness.
- **Accidental death cover** pays a set benefit if you die because of certain types of accident (as opposed to an illness or disease).

What's the difference between 'advised' life insurance and 'direct' life insurance and 'super' life insurance?

You can either buy life insurance through an adviser, or direct from an insurance company, or through your super fund.

That's the main difference - where you buy them. But there are also some product differences between the three options.

For example, ASIC data says that 'direct' life insurance has more claims rejected and more disputes than 'advised' insurance and 'super' insurance, as this table shows:

	Disputes per 100,000 lives insured	Claims accepted rate	Average claim time (months)
'Super' Life Insurance	0.7	97.9%	1.3
Direct Life Insurance	13.0	88.1%	3.1
Advised Life Insurance	5.9	97.5%	3.5

Source: ASIC Moneysmart

What is 'underwritten' life insurance?

It means they ask you a bunch of questions when you take out the policy and they give you a price based on how risky they think you are. That can be a boring half-hour at the time, but it can also mean that as long as you answer their questions truthfully, your claims are more likely to be paid (see the table above).

A fully underwritten insurance contract also ensures that you can renew each year, regardless of any change in your medical condition, without the need for further underwriting.

Most 'advised' life insurance works like this, which is why a higher percentage of those claims are paid, and some 'direct' life insurers do it too.

Most 'direct' life insurance, however, is not underwritten. It's 'one size fits all', and the downside of that seems to be that claims are rejected slightly more often.

Are some policies better than others?

Yes, of course. But only *you* can know for sure which policy suits you best. You can get help from a financial adviser or planner, or you can do your own shopping around, or you can look at the ratings on websites such as Canstar.com.au. Just remember: if you're not getting financial advice, read the PDS to see if the product is right for you.

What's the difference between 'stepped premiums' and 'level premiums'?

Just like it says: one type goes up over time, the other stays flat. Stepped premiums go up as you get older because the actuaries believe you're more likely to make a claim. The annual step-ups in premiums are relatively modest for those aged under 40 but increase substantially as we get older; up to 10% or more per annum for those aged over 60. Most cover offered by Australian life insurers features stepped premiums.

Level premiums are usually quite high at younger ages but they don't feature the big increases as you get older.

How much life insurance do I need?

Government regulator to the rescue! ASIC's Moneysmart website has a commonsense calculator to tell you how much you need. Just punch your answers in at this link:

www.moneysmart.gov.au/tools-and-resources/calculators-and-apps/life-insurance-calculator

Does my insurer pay out?

Once again, it's the regulator to the rescue! ASIC Moneysmart has a claims calculator that shows the record of various insurers when it comes to paying claims:

www.moneysmart.gov.au/tools-and-resources/calculators-and-apps/life-insurance-claims-comparison-tool

Congratulations!

You made it through life insurance and you've well and truly earned your Red Bill-Killing Belt, Grasshopper.

And you've earned one last side-splitting dad joke too: Two oranges walk into a bar. One says to the other, 'You're round.'

Now, game face on! It's finally time to take on the Big Kahuna of household bills: the home loan. You're ready.

CHAPTER 18
HOME LOANS

If you've just picked up this book and turned straight to this chapter, I like your style.

No warming up on the smaller bills and building up to the big ones for you. No ma'am. You mean business.

If you've read the book from the beginning, on the other hand, you're now the Ralph Macchio of money-saving and this is like the final fight in *The Karate Kid* where you whip out the crane kick and finish off your floppy blond-haired nemesis.

This bill is the biggest of them all. But the bigger they are, the harder they fall.

Shave a couple of percentage points off here and it could save you tens of thousands of dollars over time because thanks to our property boom, most home loans are *buuuuge* these days and they go for up to 30 years.

KILLER STAT: On an average principal and interest loan of just $300,000 over 25 years, if you can get your interest rate down from say 4.3% p.a. to 3.8% p.a. it'll save you a massive . . .

- $83 a month,
- $996 a year,
- or $24,917 over the 25-year loan!

At a glance

Potential saving	Tens of thousands of dollars over the life of your loan
Degree of difficulty	4 out of 5 (but only because of all the bloody paperwork)
Best times to save	Anytime
Time required to switch	Several hours over several days or weeks
Top online tools	Financial comparison sites such as Canstar.com.au and Finder.com.au, as well as the newer 'home loan marketplaces' like LoanDolphin.com.au and Lendi.com.au

If I could tell you one thing about Home Loans it would be:	If you're paying an interest rate that starts with a four (or God forbid, a five), you're paying too much.

QUICK BILL-KILL: Home Loans

If you haven't compared your home loan interest rate to what's out there for a year or more, you might already be blowing thousands of unnecessary dollars.

Here's a four-step guide to getting a quick saving with minimal fuss, but note that it only works if you're at least prepared to walk away, De Niro-style!

1. **Check your interest rate.** Even if you think you know it, it might have changed. It should be on a recent statement or in your internet banking profile. It should start with a '3'. (Also, check any fees such as annual package fees.)
2. **Find out the cheapest rates on the market.** You can do this by putting your loan details into a comparison site such as finder.com.au or canstar.com.au (NB: Most sites will show you 'promoted' or 'partner' offers first. Look for a link or a button that says 'show all offers' or 'show offers without links' to get the whole picture.) Or if you're happy to take calls, you can use one of the 'online mortgage

marketplaces' such as LoanDolphin.com.au or Lendi.com.au

3. **Check the comparison rate!** To stop lenders from hiding sneaky fees behind a super-low interest rate, they *must* quote this number, which boils all the major fees and charges in the first year down to a single percentage figure. It's a godsend.
4. **Time to switch or upgrade.** Got a broker? Send them the info you've just found and ask them to contact the bank and see what they can do to improve your rate. No broker? Call your lender and do it yourself: if you're armed with the above information, they should play ball. (Remember that it will cost them over $1500 to find another customer to replace you!) Use the script below if you want:

> *'Hi, my name is ______ and I've been a customer for _____ years. I've just noticed my interest rate is ______% p.a. and there are now rates out there of ______% p.a. with [insert name of competitor] and _____% p.a. with [insert name of another competitor]. So I'm planning on switching. But I just thought I'd make one final call to see if you can give me a better deal than the one I'm on. What's the best rate you can offer me to stay?'*

> Everyone loves to hear about a home loan win! Post your savings to @OneBigSwitchAU and @KillBillsBook with the hashtag #KillBills and we'll share it with all the other Bill-Killers out there.

HARD TRUTH: Why the home loan industry is like shopping in Bali

Imagine every time you went to a petrol station to fill up, they asked you your bank balance, your employment status and your spending habits, and then charged you a price based on how financially secure you are.

Because that's the hard truth when it comes to mortgages: everyone pays a different price, and just about *no one* pays the advertised rate.

Banks advertise their 'standard variable rate' (SVR) but behind the scenes, it's more like shopping in Bali: how much you pay all comes down to how well you haggle and what sort of a customer you are.

And that's the main reason why about half of all home loans in this country are sorted by a broker, I reckon. Aussies love Bali, but as I argued in Part 1 of this book, we hate to haggle! And we're more than happy to let someone else do it for us (especially if someone else is paying them and we can't get a much better result doing it ourselves).

There's also the fact that home loans are highly regulated because there are such big bucks at stake, and high regulation means lots of red tape: forms, forms and more forms.

Brokers take the pain out of the red tape and they deal with the bank so we don't have to. And there's nothing wrong with that. If you're too busy or too lazy to deal direct with your lender, a good broker's for you.

Full disclosure: I use a broker! Not because I don't think I could haggle with the bank myself, but because he does a great job of it, he's handled several irritating administrative stuff-ups for us, and importantly, I don't see any evidence that my bank would give me a better deal if we cut the middleman out.

Each of us needs to make our own decision on this one, based on what we need and how much time and energy we have for our banking.

For example, if you wanted to switch to HSBC, a big international bank that offers some of the lowest rates around, I'd contact them directly, because they don't deal with most brokers. Ditto a lot of the lenders with the cheapest rates advertised online – they're cheaper because they don't factor in the average $3000 that others pay a broker for a loan!

There are also some very sophisticated new online 'mortgage marketplaces' popping up that are essentially a 'robo-broker'. You put your details in, they scan hundreds of loans and recommend a few loans and brokers for you (more on those soon).

Lenders are working on getting the red tape down too – some application processes are now 100% online so you never have to deal with a human being, and that reduces the cost too.

These are new ways that you can now get some of the services of a broker while accessing the cheapest of the cheap. But you'll still need to do a bit of the legwork yourself.

True Story: My mortgage broker feeds my dog chicken breast

We met our broker because a real estate agent told us he'd arranged her loan. Why would a real estate agent need a broker? I thought. But over time it's become obvious how brokers can earn their keep, no matter how savvy you are about property.

First, he switched us from one bank to another. We weren't too fussed about which lender we were with as long as the rate was low. He has purchasing power with one particular big bank because he puts a lot of business through them and he's part of a network of brokers who do the same.

To some extent, interest rates are set in stone: if you borrow $X and you have $Y of equity in your home, you'll get a 1% or a 1.5% discount on the standard variable rate.

But it's an open secret in the industry that there's a tiny bit of wriggle room: when there are line-ball calls, you can make an application to the bank's 'pricing department' for a slightly better deal, and sometimes you'll get it. Good brokers know this and they know what's likely to get through and what's not. They might also have some sway with the bank if they work regularly with them.

Brokers can also come in handy when things go wrong. When our new bank sent us our new ATM cards and other info, they never arrived.

We told the broker, he contacted the bank and reordered them, and they sent them again.

This time, I got a call at about 2am on a Wednesday night to ask if I'd been spending up big at petrol stations and all-night stores in a part of Sydney about one hour from where I live.

Nope. I'd been punching out *zzzs*, I told them. But someone had been having a Paywave party on us. With our new ATM cards!

We told the broker, he contacted the bank and re-ordered them, and they sent them again.

Eventually it was all sorted out but it reminded us that banks stuff it up sometimes, and it can help to have someone with a direct line and some clout to help fix them.

These days, our broker makes donations to our kids' school fundraisers, invites them for swims in his pool and feeds my dog chicken breast.

He's sorted out several administrative shemozzles like this over the years and he's haggled them down to a lower rate on about three occasions, ensuring that we've almost always had something that starts with a '3'.

He's getting paid by the bank to keep us happy and that's fine with me (and with Sunny, my dog) for now.

The best insider tricks to use on . . . home loans

The De Niro

Unless you've turned straight to this chapter, you'll know all about this trick by now. The De Niro is an attitude. It's about playing hard to get. As in most industries, it's the borrowers who are *prepared to switch* who get the best results – even if you end up staying put.

Switching rates in banking are far too low. Governments for years have talked a good game about fixing this but at the end of the day, Australians have decided it's still a hassle.

The banks know this and they 'bank' on you staying put. But if you're prepared to move, then you can take the upper hand – because this is one industry where there are more than 50 different options to choose from!

KILLER STAT: We're more likely to get divorced than to break up with our bank, and about 40% of us are still with the first bank we ever opened an account with.

Comparison site RateCity.com.au has looked at this in the past and found that new customers on average received interest rates that were 1.11% cheaper than loyal 'old' customers - which adds up to $70,000 over the life of a $300,000 30-year home loan. Ouch!

True Stories: There are De Niros giving their banks hell all over the place. Just ask around

I did a little experiment while writing this chapter. I whacked the following question up on Facebook just to see how many De Niros there were out there playing hardball with their lenders.

'Anyone had success negotiating their mortgage lender down to a lower rate - or switching to another lender - recently? I'm writing something about home loans and keen to hear people's experiences.'

I might as well have asked who makes the best coffee in Melbourne. I was inundated.

My buddy Joanne: 'Yep. Two or three times. CBA. We just ring and ask for an extra discount every now and then and they reluctantly agree. Weird.'

My old workmate Nick: 'Commonwealth ignored my query, so we went to a smaller bank, IMB, that massively undercut them and did all the legwork for me. Current rate is 3.59%. Earlier one was well over 4. Let's have a red wine lunch later in winter!'

My old high school pal Dave: 'Hey, mate. So every year we review. We originally got our loan through a broker. It is with Citibank and is a full service loan. Last year, we got an offer from a new broker for a much better rate. I called Citi and within 20 mins they dropped the rate from 3.93% to 3.69%. They moved rates up in January to 3.85% and last month HSBC approached us with a rate of 3.75%. So I called Citi again and they dropped the rate again to 3.79%. We will now check every six months!'

My brother's mate Jared: 'I had two mortgages with Westpac for over 12 years and moved to HSBC for a new purchase . . . Westpac failed to match so I subsequently moved my other mortgage products to HSBC out of principle.'

My friend Amber: 'We have our home loan with NAB. [My husband's] business does their banking with CBA and they approached him with an offer if we moved our home loan to them – they would reduce our interest rate and have zero fees. We took that to NAB and basically said "Match this or we walk" and they matched it.'

And this – equally inspirational if not very helpful – from my dad: 'Getting rid of a mortgage is a great feeling.'

The Moving Target

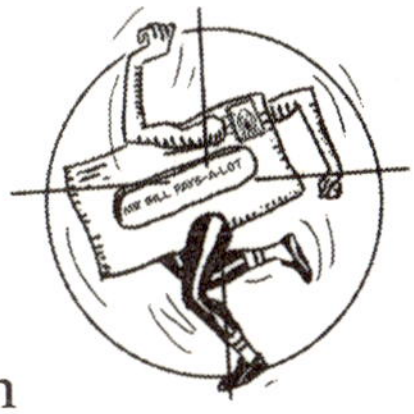

The Reserve Bank of Australia has been dropping the official interest rate from 'record low' to new 'record low' since 2015. In mid-2016 it hit 1.50% p.a. And in 2019 it started dropping further. As I write this it's 1.25% p.a. By the time you read this, it will probably be lower.

But don't be fooled. Banks' rates have still been up and down like a bride's nightie in recent years, despite the cash rate heading consistently down, down, down.

My own rate rose by 0.90% in one year, for example, because of a clampdown on interest-only lending.

Meanwhile, some lenders have dropped the rates on certain loans to their own 'record lows' to try and attract the 'best' sort of customers: refinancers who own more than 20% equity in their home, want to pay principal and interest, and have stable employment.

So in recent years it's become a 'refinancer's market', and that means that if you're already in the market, you're a real catch for a bank.

The Moving Target Trick is designed to cash in on bills where the price changes regularly, and home loans are one of those bills.

So don't just 'set and forget' this one. It could cost you a packet. If there's *one* bill you're going to shop around for once a year, make it this one.

David's Slingshot

Unlike insurance, where you can't really compare prices online, home loan options are very easy to navigate on the internet.

This bill gets more complicated once you start applying for loans and you have to deal with qualification processes and paperwork, but the first bit - taking a look at what's out there - is easy.

You've got a few options:

Slingshot #1. Comparison websites

Just go to one of the bigger comparison sites (three examples listed below), punch in your details, and see what they kick out.

You'll need to decide what 'features' you can't do without. Need an offset account? Some loans don't have them. A redraw facility? Ditto. Not prepared to leave the big banks? Be prepared to pay a bit more for

TIGHTARSE TIP: Most sites will show you 'promoted' or 'partner' offers first. Look for a link or a button that says 'show all offers' or 'show offers without links' to get the whole picture.

the privilege. Once you know your non-negotiables, you can adjust your search accordingly.

Remember to look at the 'Comparison Rates'. These are a godsend from regulators because they adjust the advertised interest rate to include any other fees that apply on the loan in the first year.

These sites really are very easy to use, and they often have special offers on them too that are even better than the standard deal. These are three of the biggest:

WEBSITE	RANGE
Finder.com.au	Compares 60 plus lenders
Canstar.com.au	Compares 100 plus lenders
Ratecity.com.au	Compares 100 plus lenders

As you'll see in the Quick home loans 'Bill-Kill' above, a bit of up-to-date info about the other offers out there is the key to getting a better deal.

Slingshot #2. 'Robo-brokers'

If you don't want to hunt around on a comparison site for interest rates, and you don't have a good broker to do it for you, there's a range of new tools you can try out. Let's call them 'Robo-brokers'.

Technology catches up with all of us eventually, and now it's evolving in the mortgage business too, as web developers race to replace human brokers with these 'online home loan marketplaces' that collect your data and then shop *you* around to brokers and lenders.

> **INSIDE INFO:** You can't just browse loans and kick the tyres on these sites like you can on the comparison websites above. Robo-brokers ask a lot of questions before they will show you your results, so you'll need some time up your sleeve (say, 20 minutes) and you'll need to give most of them your number and take a call.

One of the advantages of these platforms is that - like a real broker - once they know a bit about you they can hunt down loans that you're likely to be approved for. Chances are you won't know this yourself when browsing the cheapest loans on comparison websites above, and many of those cheapest loans are only available to the most desirable lenders.

So if you're serious about finding a low rate and you don't want to do your own searching, by all means give one of these guys a go. They're a great way to find a broker, for example. I made inquiries with the ones below for research purposes and within minutes I had several offers of loans with comparison rates below 4.00% p.a.

Once you get an offer from them, the power is in your hands: you can either take it up or see if your current lender will match it:

LoanDolphin:
www.loandolphin.com.au
PROS:

- Over $100 million in home loan auctions done already.
- You'll see the rates, the lenders and the brokers' details on a single dashboard.

CONS:

- Their process asks you a lot of questions so you'll need all your info handy - your income, your expenses and so on. These are home loans, after all . . . But it's still quicker than going to a bank or meeting with a broker upfront.

Lendi:
www.lendi.com.au
PROS:

- More than $5 billion in loans settled already.
- You can do the entire home loan application process online if you want to.
- More than 30 lenders are compared.

CONS:

- Their longwinded process also asks you a lot of questions, including an ID check that requires a photo and licence or passport. But again, it's quicker than doing it in person somewhere so if that suits you, then try it out.

HashChing:
www.hashching.com.au
PROS:

- Over $1 billion in loans processed already.
- 300 plus certified brokers are on the platform.
- More than 40 lenders are compared.
- Has its own customer rating system for brokers.

CONS:

- They show you the rates, but not the lenders until you request a callback from a broker.

True Story: How Jess saved $1500 p.a. on her rent with a single email

I've concentrated on homeowners in this book but most of these tricks work for renters too. For example, my colleague Jess Tancred used some of these strategies and saved $1500 a year on her rent.

Jess used the internet to research similar properties (David's Slingshot and The Mystery-Shopper), said she wanted to negotiate before she'd renew the lease (The De Niro), and wrote a very polite whinge to her real estate agent (The Squeaky Wheel) which she's allowed me to share below:

> 'Hi Katherine,
>
> Prior to renewing my lease I would like to discuss the possibility of a rent negotiation.
>
> I have done some research online and seen Unit 5 used images from my apartment and is leased for $495 per week, $55 less per week than what I pay.
>
> Similarly Unit 4, albeit not at the same standard as mine, is asking for $100 less per week than my apartment. It is however in the same location, the same size with the exact same amenities.
>
> I take excellent care of the apartment, pay my rent on time and I'm a respectable and considerate neighbour and tenant.
>
> I believe a deduction of $30 per week is a fair and reasonable amount.

Could you please let me know if the landlord is willing to accept this offer.

Please also let me know if you would prefer to discuss this over the phone.

Kind regards,

Jessica'

It worked! The key to Jess's win was the same as it is when negotiating with a mortgage lender: simple numbers. If it costs them less to keep you than it does to replace you with a new customer, they'd be mad to let you walk.

A new customer for a mortgage lender or a landlord costs over $1000 and often over $1500 in marketing dollars and other charges, so it just made dollars and sense for them to say yes.

The Squeaky Wheel

Remember the rule from Part 1 – to whinge well, you need to first ask for a manager and, if that fails, then escalate to polite public whingeing and finally whingeing to the regulator.

All financial product providers have to have an internal dispute resolution process and, if that doesn't work, they're subject to regulation by the Australian Financial Complaints Authority, AFCA.

Since 2018, all new financial services complaints are dealt with by these guys. You can contact them on 1800 931 678 or visit their website: www.afca.org.au

AFCA can conciliate between you and the provider, they can ask for further information to help deal with your complaint, and they can make a decision that's binding on the provider, if it's accepted by you.

Note that they can't consider a complaint about a bog-standard fee or interest rate increase, unless it falls into one of the categories below.

Here's what they *can* accept complaints about:

- Fees or charges that were incorrectly applied or calculated (but not if your only concern is that you believe the fee or charge was too high).
- Information that you weren't given about the product or that you were given and you believe was misleading or incorrect, including fees or costs.
- If you're in financial difficulty and can't make repayments.
- Decisions that your financial firm has made, including a decision to pursue an unpaid debt and whether a decision to lend was made responsibly.
- If you gave instructions and they weren't followed.
- Privacy and confidentiality breaches.
- Transactions that were incorrect or unauthorised, or mistaken payments.

6 other ways to save on home loans

1. **Have an offset account:** Not all loans feature this but many do. All it means is that you have an account (say, your savings or main transaction account) where the balance counts towards your mortgage, as if you've already paid it onto the mortgage. Therefore it reduces the amount you pay interest on while still giving you access to the money if you need it.
2. **Have a redraw facility:** This is very similar to an offset account, except it works the other way. You can take back money you've paid onto the mortgage, if you need it.
3. **Pay more than you have to:** It's surprising how much an extra $100 a week or so can make your mortgage disappear more quickly. If you can afford to pay more than the minimum principal and interest payment your bank requires, do it. Make sure you're allowed to first (some fixed rate loans forbid it, for example). ASIC Moneysmart gives the following example:

Case Study: Jie and Ming save $65,000 and four years by paying extra

Let's say a young couple borrows $380,000 over 25 years at 6% p.a. (Not a good rate, but it's just a hypothetical example created by the financial watchdog's 'Moneysmart' website . . .)

'Jie and Ming then realised that by making slightly higher repayments fortnightly (calculated by dividing the monthly payment by two), they would end up making an extra monthly payment each year.

'This would mean they could pay off the loan four years early and save about $65,000 in interest.'

Google 'ASIC mortgage calculator' to see how much you could shave off your loan by paying extra:

www.moneysmart.gov.au/tools-and-resources/calculators-and-apps/mortgage-calculator#!how-can-i-repay-my-loan-sooner

4. **Exercise your NEW 'consumer data right':** This is a new right you have, starting from 2019, to access your banking data and show it to anyone you like. The idea is that you'll be able to request a file from Bank A and show it to Bank B to ask them what is the best offer they'd be prepared to make to you. It's early days, but this new 'open banking' rule could transform the way we shop around for not just home loans, but also energy and telco (the next bills on the 'consumer data right' list). So watch this space!

   More info here: www.accc.gov.au/focus-areas/consumer-data-right-cdr-0
5. **Go interest-only (short-term solution only!):** This will end up costing you more over the long run but if you've hit a rough patch where your income

has dropped, one option is to move to an interest-only loan for a period of time. These became very popular from about 2010 to 2015 before regulators cracked down on them, so it's now harder to get approved and the rates are not as low as principal and interest loans. But because you're paying interest only, the repayments could be lower on these loans. Ask your broker or your bank first.

6. **Ask your bank for relief (short-term solution only!):** If you're in financial trouble, every lender is required to have a 'hardship program' for people like you. Make sure you talk to them if you've missed a repayment or you're likely to, so they know why - and what they can do to help you get back on track.

   ASIC Moneysmart says these are the steps you need to apply for a 'hardship variation':

   1. Contact your lender or credit provider - by phone or in writing.
   2. Ask to speak to a 'hardship officer' or to 'customer service'.
   3. Give the details of your loan (account name and number, and the amount you pay each week/fortnight/month).
   4. Say that you want to change your loan repayments because you are experiencing hardship (as set out in section 72 of the National Consumer Credit Code).
   5. Explain why you are having difficulties making payments, how long you think your financial problems will continue and how much you can afford to repay.

The Financial Rights Legal Centre also creates sample letters you can use as a template at this address: financialrights.org.au/sample-letters/

If you are not satisfied with the lender's response you can contact the Australian Financial Complaints Authority (afca.org.au) on 1800 931 678. This is a free external dispute resolution scheme.

7. **If you're a first home buyer, access your government freebies:** Since 2000, many first home buyers have been able to access a First Home Owner Grant from their state government. Eligibility varies from state to state and the rules change regularly so check them at firsthome.gov.au. At the time of writing they were:

   In NSW: $10,000 for the purchase or building of new homes valued at $750,000 or less, plus a waiver of stamp duty for homes (new or otherwise) under $800,000.

   In Qld: $15,000 for the purchase or building of new homes valued at less than $750,000.

   In Vic: $10,000 for the purchase or building of new homes (or $20,000 in regional Victoria) valued at $750,000 or less, plus a waiver of some stamp duty for homes (new or otherwise).

   In SA: $15,000 for the purchase or building of new homes valued at up to $575,000.

   In WA: $10,000 for the purchase or building of new homes valued at up to $750,000 or $1million (depending on where the home is).

In the ACT: The grant ended in July 2019. Check the website above for updates.

In the NT: $20,000 for the purchase or build of new homes for the first 600 applicants for the BuildBonus grant launched in 2019, plus up to $18,601 off stamp duty for the purchase of a home (new or otherwise).

From January 2020, there should also be a new First Home Loan Deposit Scheme which means some first home buyers will only have to save 5% deposit instead of 20% (more on that below).

Everything you wanted to know about home loans (and then some . . .)

How much do I need to save to buy my first home?

Ideally you need 20% of the purchase price. That's because if you have to borrow more than 80% of the price, you'll need lender's mortgage insurance, which adds another cost, and some lenders might even charge you a higher interest rate.

The exception to this rule is if you qualify for the new First Home Loan Deposit Scheme announced by Prime Minister Scott Morrison during the 2019 election campaign.

Under this $500 million plan, 10,000 first home buyers with an income of up to $125,000 a year (or $200,000 for couples) will be able to purchase properties of a certain price from January 2020 with only a 5% deposit and the National Housing Finance and Investment Corporation will go guarantor for the remaining 15% so that they can avoid Lender's Mortgage Insurance.

Not everyone is a fan of buying with a low deposit, however. ASIC's Moneysmart, the Captain Sensible of money websites, says: 'The bigger your deposit, the less you have to borrow, and the more you will save in interest.'

Remember to factor in all the other nasty little surprises like stamp duty, legal fees, land tax, rates, home insurance and any windfalls such as the Australian Government's First Home Owner Grant.

Should I apply for a fixed rate or a variable rate?

This will sound like a cop-out, but it's up to you. A fixed rate is locked in for a certain period of time and you pay a fee if you want to get out of it. A variable rate changes when the bank wants to change it but you're not locked in.

As the likes of Barefoot Investor Scott Pape have pointed out, simple mathematics suggests you'll lose more often than you'll win on fixed rates. The bank's in-house geeks have spent many long hours calculating what fixed rates they can offer that will look attractive, but will make the bank more money over the two, three or five years than a variable rate is likely to make. In other words, take the fixed rate and you're betting against the bank's top brains. It's like the casino; the house (almost) always wins.

This happened to us the last time we fixed half our mortgage for a few years: the RBA started cutting rates again and we'll probably lose the bet with the bank in the end.

But I've always liked fixing at least part of our loan so that you can budget for what it's going to cost you over the next little while. It minimises surprises. A lot of people hedge their bets in this way - fix about half your loan and leave half variable.

In the end, this one depends largely on what sort of person you are. Do whatever makes you happy! Just make sure - whether fixed or variable - that it's a good rate.

How do rate discounts work?

The big banks offer 'standard variable' home loan rates (SVRs) starting with a '5' or a '4', which you can reduce to a '4' or a '3' by taking out one of their 'wealth packages' and/or by taking out a large loan. The package fee is usually about $400 and it gets you a discount of anywhere between 1% and 2% (aka 100 basis points to 200 basis points) depending on how much you borrow. It sometimes also gets you other benefits such as fewer fees on your loans, transaction accounts or credit cards, and insurance discounts. It's their #1 way of keeping all your financial products in the one place.

Broker or no broker?

I've explained above why I use a broker, but also why it's not necessary for some people. I think this one also depends on what sort of person you are, and what your current circumstances are. Confident haggler? Internet savvy? Like your smaller, challenger brands and keen to kiss the Big Four goodbye? Well then, it sounds like you're the 'no broker' type to me, especially if you have the time to research online and deal direct with your lender.

Hate haggling? Not computer-savvy? Or super-busy with a young family and no time for admin? Maybe a broker's for you. Here are some of the *pros* and *cons* of using a broker:

PROs:

- **Discounts:** Brokers can sometimes get a better deal than you from certain lenders because they buy 'wholesale'. The flipside of this is that they often steer you towards the lenders they prefer to deal with (or who pay them more). So they may not compare the whole market for you. (In fact, they almost certainly won't compare lenders who don't pay brokers!)
- **Paperwork:** Brokers take care of a lot of the red tape involved in a loan application, which can be mind-numbingly boring and time-consuming for those of us who don't deal with it day-in, day-out.
- **Customer service:** Brokers are middlemen and middlewomen. They save you time comparing loans and

when dealing with banks and other lenders, it can be a relief to have someone in your corner to stick up for you or push their weight around if need be.

CONs:

- **Control:** Brokers' commissions get bigger according to how much business they can send to a particular lender. So using a broker might mean you're channelled towards a particular product, when you wanted someone to compare the whole market for you.
- **Risk:** Brokers' clients tend to borrow more and take on more risky loans such as interest-only loans, according to research by ASIC. This may be because brokers are paid according to the size of the loan so it's in their interest for you to borrow more.
- **Cost:** Brokers get over $2b in commissions a year and that adds 16 basis points to the cost of the average home loan, according to a UBS report. (On the other hand, in most cases you pay that extra amount whether you use a broker or not, so you might as well get the free service unless you're dealing with a lender that does not pay brokers . . .)

What should I ask a broker at our first meeting?

1. How many lenders do you deal with?
2. Which lender do you put the most loans through and why?
3. What are the upfront costs of the loan?

4. Are you a member of the MFAA? (The peak body for mortgage brokers in Australia, which requires members to abide by a Code of Practice.)
5. I just found an interest rate of [insert low rate] at the comparison website [insert website name]. Can you beat that?

Should I refinance?

It's really important to do a sense-check on your loan about once a year but bear in mind that it's not always a great time to refinance. The pros include accessing a lower rate; accessing equity in your home to renovate, invest or buy something; and maybe paying off the loan faster. Or your life might have changed and you might just need a feature you didn't need before such as an offset account or a redraw facility or a line-of-credit home loan.

On the other hand, it costs money to close out one loan and open another, so check the costs with a broker or the lender and factor that in. The fees can include:

- discharge fee, to get out of your old loan: $200–$400;
- exit fee (if you took our your loan before July 2011, or you have a fixed rate loan): can cost thousands;
- application/establishment fees for the new loan: $200–$600;
- valuation fees, to pay an independent valuer to assess the property: $300;
- settlement fees, for the lender to arrange the funding: $100–$300;

- legal fees, for the lender's solicitor: $75–$150;
- package fees, a monthly cost that some lenders charge in exchange for giving you a discount on the variable rate: $100–$500;
- lender's mortgage insurance, if you're borrowing over 80% of the property value: can cost thousands.

> **TIGHTARSE TIP:** Sometimes a new lender will cover or waive some of these fees just to win you over, so be sure to ask them. You're never more attractive than when you're a potential new customer!

You made it. You're a Black Belt in killing bills.

If you're reading this, and you didn't skip to this page, that means you've earnt your money-saving Black Belt, and you're now a bona fide Bill-Killer.

Bills will fear you, your family will thank you, and friends will love you for the tips you can now give them. You might even become like me – another person who talks about power bills at barbecues. (Just what the world needs!)

Go forth and kick some serious household bill butt, my friend, and thank you for reading.

PART 3

RECOMMENDED BOOKS & WEBSITES

WEBSITES & APPS

OneBigSwitch.com.au - This is where I work. We use the People Power of over one million Australians who have joined up since 2011 to negotiate group discounts on household bills. It's free to join. Get on board.

9Saver.com.au - One Big Switch's sister site, this is a partnership with Nine so you'll see 9Saver popping up regularly with savings tips and special offers on *TODAY*, *A Current Affair* and other Nine programs.

FiftyUpClub.com.au - One Big Switch's other sister site, this is a partnership with Macquarie Media and can be heard on stations such as 2GB, 3AW, 4BC and 6PR.

Canstar.com.au - Australia's 'biggest' (i.e. most comprehensive) comparison site, with over 700 brands compared. They also have a system of awards and star ratings that help you work out which brands are the real deal and which ones are pretenders.

Finder.com.au - Australia's 'most-visited' comparison site. Started with credit cards and has branched out to cover multiple products. These guys specialise in content: they've got articles on just about any question you could want answered on money and personal finance.

BarefootInvestor.com - If you like what you read in Scott Pape's bestseller, you can join his email database and get free weekly updates from him.

OzBargain.com.au - Australia's #1 online community for hardcore hunters of 'deals, vouchers, coupons, discounts and freebies'. Community members post everything from home loan deals they've spotted to discounts on KFC, then the deals get ranked according to how many like them. I thought I was into money-saving until I visited this site but their dedication to killing bills is on a whole different level!

SpendingHacker.com.au - A long-running savings blog. It's not pretty, but it's been around for years and it's run by Michael Ginsburg, who knows his stuff and does a lot of research into products that can save the average household big bucks. It's also free.

SavingsGuide.com.au - Another long-running savings blog, run by a husband and wife team who have done some work for us in the past. They've put together a bunch of savings hacks and challenges for those who want to save more and spend less. Worth a look.

EnergyMadeEasy.gov.au - The government website for comparing electricity and gas deals across NSW, South-east Qld, and SA. It's very good - except for locating 'under-the-table deals', which are often not on these sites. But more people should use this website as a starting point for saving on power bills.

Compare.energy.vic.gov.au - The government website for comparing electricity and gas deals across Victoria. Same as above - it's also very good, except for locating 'under-the-table deals'.

EnergySwitch.service.nsw.gov.au - A NSW government website where you can upload your last email bill and it will compare most of the electricity and gas deals across NSW for you. It's early days but tools like this are the future when it comes to finding cheaper electricity.

PrivateHealth.gov.au - The government website for comparing all the health insurance deals available across Australia. It's comprehensive but it's clunky so unless you're determined to do it all yourself, use one of the commercial sites below.

iSelect.com.au - The biggest commercial comparison website in Australia, they built their business by helping people save on health insurance. They don't compare all providers, but they really know their stuff, and it's a free service.

MembersOwn.com.au - A smaller commercial comparison site that only compares not-for-profit health funds. Most of these are not compared at the bigger sites such as iSelect, so it's also worth a look.

ACCC.gov.au - The competition and consumer watchdog's website has all sorts of useful info, particularly on their pet topics of petrol, the NBN and online shopping. They've also got extensive information on your consumer rights, from how to complain, to warranties, product safety and scams!

Moneysmart.gov.au - This is the corporate regulator ASIC's consumer info website, and it's chock-a-block full of information (maybe too much information!) on everything from insurance to banking, credit and super. But the best reason to visit is the dozens of tools: mortgage switching calculators, credit card calculators, retirement calculators, and apps to help you buy a car, track your spend or cultivate good saving habits.

FinancialRights.gov.au - The Financial Rights Legal Centre offers free advice and advocacy for consumers who are in financial stress. There are sample letters, fact sheets, a National Debt Helpline and a tool to use if you're in a car crash and you need to work out what to do next.

AFCA.org.au - The Australian Financial Complaints Authority is a newish super-ombudsman for credit, banking, insurance, investments and superannuation complaints. If you've tried to get a resolution from your provider and had no luck, this is the place to go next.

Ombudsman.gov.au - The Commonwealth Ombudsman deals with a range of complaints and health insurance is one of their areas. They publish a bunch of fact sheets and brochures, they run the government comparison website and they have an independent complaint-handling service.

TIO.com.au - TIO is your new best friend if you've tried and failed to get a problem with your telco fixed. The Telecommunications Industry Ombudsman is industry-funded but independently governed, and it can make enforceable decisions about complaints up to $50,000, and make recommendations up to $100,000.

Your local Energy Ombudsman - This is where to go if you have a dispute with your power company and you haven't been able to get a resolution by contacting the provider first.

- NSW Energy & Water Ombudsman: www.ewon.com.au/
- Energy & Water Ombudsman Victoria: www.ewov.com.au/

- Energy & Water Ombudsman Queensland: www.ewoq.com.au/
- Energy & Water Ombudsman SA: ewosa.com.au/
- Energy & Water Ombudsman WA: www.ombudsman.wa.gov.au/energyandwater/
- Energy Ombudsman Tasmania: www.energyombudsman.tas.gov.au/
- Energy Ombudsman ACT: www.acat.act.gov.au/

RECOMMENDED READING

Scott Pape, *The Barefoot Investor* - If you're one of a handful of people who haven't read this book yet (it's sold over a million copies), it's a publishing phenomenon. Scott helps readers to organise their basic financial lives, pay down debt and set themselves up for the future. It's like Financial Planning 101, but with bonus dad jokes and lots of attitude.

Effie Zahos, *A Real Girl's Guide to Money: From Converse to Louboutins* - Effie started and edited *Money Magazine* for many years. She's an excellent communicator and really knows her stuff. This book is clearly aimed at - and has really hit the mark with - younger professional women.

David Koch, *Kochie's 11-Step Money Plan for a Better Life* - Sunrise host and finance commentator David Koch finally wrote a book recently too. It's a real nuts-and-bolts guide to balancing the household budget and establishing good habits that could save you big bucks over the years.

Anita Bell, *Your Mortgage and How to Pay It Off in Five Years (By Someone Who Did It in Three)* – This one's a best-seller from the noughties and is a great resource for first-home buyers. It's a bit outdated, of course – property is much more expensive now, for one! But still a good one for the bill-killer's library.

Barry Schwartz, *The Paradox of Choice: Why More Is Less* – A think-y book by an American psychologist who says that we have so much choice in our modern lives that we often get paralysed by all the options and end up doing nothing – the worst possible option. I love his message to all the perfectionists out there: relax! 'Good enough' is almost always good enough.

Richard Thaler & Cass Sunstein, *Nudge: Improving Decisions about Health, Wealth, and Happiness* – One of the authors is a Nobel Prize-winning behavioural economist, so this book was hugely influential. It's all about human nature and how businesses and governments can understand it and use that knowledge to 'nudge' us to act a certain way. There are now official 'nudge' units in many of the western world's governments.

PART 4

THE HALF-A-DOZEN-BILL-KILL: SAVE OVER $1000 IN AN AFTERNOON

This section is for the busy, the bored, or the just plain lazy. If you haven't got the time or the energy to read the rest of this book, but you want to try for a quick and dirty saving of $1000 or more in a morning or an afternoon, you've come to the right place.

There's a short 'Bill-Kill' in each chapter of this book for the nine major household bills we've covered.

Here, I concentrate on the low-hanging fruit and condense it into the 'Half-a-Dozen-Bill-Kill': a handful of common bills, a few hours max, $1000-plus in potential savings.

Start the clock. Here goes nothing ...

BILL #1: Energy

- Grab your last electricity bill. It should tell you your usage over the most recent quarter or month, the rates you're paying, and what discount you're getting. If you've got solar, it might also say what Feed-in Tariff (FiT) they pay you.
- Go to the government website energymadeeasy.gov.au (or compare.energy.vic.gov.au in Victoria or energyswitch.service.nsw.gov.au in NSW) and enter

your details. They will show you a list of deals ranked from cheapest to most expensive. Pick the one you like the look of most out of the top three. (Note this only works in South-east Qld, NSW, Vic and SA where switching is possible.)

- Next, go to OneBigSwitch.com.au (where I work) and see what the current group-discounted deal is in your state. Reason: these don't always show up on the government website because they're not available to the general public.
- You've now got two super-cheap offers in your hand and you're ready to kill this bill. At this point, you can pick a winner and switch or you can call your provider (if you're fond of them) and ask them to beat what you've found. Here's your basic script:

> *'Hi there, my name is [Your Name Here]. I've been a loyal customer of yours for ______ years and I'd like to stay on, but I've just received two really good offers from other providers and I think they might be better than the one I'm on. ______ has offered me ______ and ______ has offered me ______. I wondered whether you can beat it? If you can, I'll lock it in right now. Perhaps you could put me through to someone on your Retention Team to see if they can help?'*

Once you decide whether to stay or switch, it will take about five minutes to fill out the form. You'll be amazed how easy it is.

Typical saving: $100–$400.

KILLER STAT: Some homes that haven't shopped around are paying as much as $2675 more than they have to for electricity, according to research by Vinnies! But it's never been easier to find a cheap deal thanks to new rules governing energy deals that came in on 1 July 2019.

- If you didn't just sign up to a dual fuel deal and you've got a gas bill, repeat the process above for natural gas and you can also save typically $50–$200 a year. (NB: this works in all the same states as for electricity, *plus* it works in WA. If you're in WA, use the website energybot.com.au to compare current gas deals available as they're not on the other sites I've listed above.)

BILL #2: Telco

- Two bills down. Now let's see if your mobile deal is up to scratch. This will only take a few minutes. First, check your current plan so you know what you're comparing to: What do you pay each month? What's your data download limit? What else is included (Calls? Phone?) Which mobile network is it on? Are you off-contract?

- Go to WhistleOut.com.au. Enter your info – data limits, inclusions and network (if you want a particular network for some reason – but otherwise select 'any'). They'll show you some options. (NB: They might show a couple of 'featured' ones first who pay for the top spot, but then they'll rank the rest from cheapest to most expensive.)
- Look at the top three to five options and pick one that you like the look of. Don't worry too much about making the perfect decision: mobile is one bill where they're all selling pretty much the same thing and you can take your number with you!

INSIDE INFO: ALL mobile plans in Australia run on either the Telstra or the Optus or the Vodafone networks, so you don't need to pay big-brand prices for big-brand coverage. In fact, you can get Telstra coverage for Aldi prices, or Optus coverage for Coles prices . . .

- If you're happy to switch, you can just sign up to the plan you've picked in minutes online. But if you really like your current provider, call them up and ask them to beat it. (Guess what? The script to use is the same as the one for energy bills above.)
- On a roll? Repeat the process above for your broadband bill if you're not currently on a contract. Ask the

mobile provider you chose if they offer a discount for you to take out your broadband with them too.

Typical saving: $50–$100 a year on mobile and $100–$200 a year on broadband.

BILL #3: Credit cards

Credit cards are the hidden household bill. The average balance is about $3500 and the average interest rate about 20% p.a. That adds up to about $700 a year. So if you don't pay it off every month, switch to a balance transfer card and pay it off, or at least switch to a low rate card and save hundreds on interest. Here's how.

- If you chose the balance transfer option, go to finder.com.au and click on 'Balance Transfer Cards'. You can sometimes pay *no* interest on the balance you move across for up to about two years! Ideally, pick one that also has a low or *no* annual fee and a low or *no* 'balance transfer fee'.
- If you picked the low rate card option, you can sometimes pay below 9% p.a. Google 'Community First Credit Union Low Rate Credit Card' or 'American

INSIDE INFO: Most comparison sites do not display these cheap-as-chips credit cards (the card providers make so little money off them that they usually don't pay others commission for selling them – which is exactly what you're looking for!).

Express Low Rate Credit Card' or check out canstar.com.au/credit-cards/low-rate-credit-cards/

- Pick a winning card, transfer your balance, move any direct debits you have set up onto your new card, lose the old card and chop it up. Leave the new card in the freezer and try not to use it. Ever.

Typical saving: $300 a year. More if you never use it again!

Take a quick bio-break. Make yourself a coffee or a tea. Eat a muffin. You deserve it. Post what you've saved on social media and bask in the Bill-Killing glory.

BILL #4: Car insurance

Now let's see what you can save on car insurance. Grab your last renewal so you have all the details of the policy.

- Go to your own insurer's website. Get an online quote using *most* of the same details as your current policy but change just enough to make yourself unrecognisable, Groucho-Marx style (you might have to use a different address or licence plate as they will probably have yours saved).
- Next, go to one of the 'challenger brand' websites such as budgetdirect.com.au or youi.com.au (up to you which one – they're both generally pretty cheap). Get a quick quote using the same details as your renewal.
- Now decide: do you want to switch or give your insurer a chance to keep you? If you want to give them a chance, the script for this one is similar but with a twist:

'Hi, my name's [Your name here] and I've been a loyal customer of yours for ______ years. I couldn't help noticing that you're charging me ______ more than you're charging a new customer with similar details to me. I know this because I got a quote on your website for a new policy with my details and I must have accidentally put my neighbour's address in. Whoops! Anyway, the quote came in at $_____. I've also got a quote from another insurer called _____ and it's only $_____. I'd like you to match or beat those other quotes, please, and if you can I'll renew right now. If you can't, I'm tempted to take my business elsewhere.'

INSIDE INFO: Even if you've paid for the year, you're not locked in. You can always switch and ask for a refund of part of your premium, based on how many months are left in the year.

Typical saving: $100–$400 a year.

BILL #5: Home insurance

Still on a roll? Use the same process above for your home insurance and see if you can save about the same amount. Or ask the car insurer you've ended up with what they'll offer you to take out home insurance with them too.

Typical saving: $100–$400 a year.

BILL #6: Home loan

Now, take a deep breath. You've already smashed up to six bills but nothing as big as this next one. The home loan is the Godzilla of household bills but you're well and truly warmed up by now. (If you're a renter, stick around. This process can work for you too.)

> **KILLER STAT:** It costs a mortgage provider more than $1000 and often over $1500 in advertising and other costs for each new customer they attract. So if they're thinking straight, they should be prepared to give you hundreds in savings to stop you leaving.

- Check your current home loan interest rate. Even if you think you know it, it might have changed. It should be on a recent statement or in your internet banking profile.
- Go to canstar.com.au or finder.com.au and check what the cheapest rates on the market are.
- If you're happy to take calls from brokers, put your details in at the online mortgage marketplaces loan-dolphin.com.au or lendi.com.au and see what deals they offer you.

- OK, time to decide: switch or negotiate. If you're not ready to switch yet, call your lender or your broker and tell them what you've been offered elsewhere. If you're armed with the above information, most times they'll play ball. If they don't, they probably don't deserve your business. You know the drill by now, soldier:

> *'Hi, my name is ______ and I've been a customer for ______ years. I've just noticed my interest rate is ______% p.a. and there are now rates out there of ______% p.a. with _____ and _____% p.a. with _____. So I'm planning on switching. But I just thought I'd make one call to see if you can match it before I do. What's the best rate you can offer me to stay?'*

Typical saving: $500–$2000 a year. It all depends how big your mortgage is and how much you get the rate down.

Renting? I haven't forgotten you! You just need to follow the same process but look for similar homes nearby on the market or recent listings to use as your other examples. Then contact your agent and ask for a rent negotiation based on the numbers. As always, you've got to be prepared to walk if it comes to that. Go to Chapter 18 to see how my workmate Jess did exactly that and saved $1500 a year on her rent.

If these strategies helped you, it's important you tell the world about them. Why? Because it'll inspire others to have a go and, like you, they'll realise what's possible and hopefully they'll never look back.

So tell a friend. Spread the word. Buy them a book or lend them this one.

And let us know too! Post your savings to @ OneBigSwitchAU and @KillBillsBook with the hashtag #KillBills and we'll share it with all the other Bill-Killers out there. We're all in this together.

ACKNOWLEDGMENTS

This book never would have made it all the way into your hands without the support of some key people.

One Big Switch's co-founder and CEO, Lachlan Harris, loves a big idea and he backed it from the moment I proposed it. He was also the first person to push me in front of a TV camera so he's got a lot to answer for.

My colleagues at RevTech Media all contributed one way or another, from finding members who saved, to sharing their experiences and covering for me while I was writing.

Former CEO David Issa and consumer campaigner Christopher Zinn taught me about 10% of what they know and that was enough for half a book.

The team at Simon & Schuster believed in this book more than any other publisher we spoke to, so thank you to Dan, Brandon, Siobhan and everyone who's had a role in getting it onto as many kitchen tables around Australia as we could.

Jessica Dettmann, Nathan Besser, Jeanne Ryckmans, Joel Naoum and Peter Banki gave invaluable early advice. Tim Dick, Sacha Molitorisz and Ian Town pitched in later on.

My wife Louise was a constant source of encouragement and, like most of my family and friends, (though they may not realise it yet!) she unwittingly provided plenty of the material in here.

Thank you also to everyone else who agreed to be quoted or tell their stories - from celebs to fabulous nobodies who love to get a win in the war on bills.

But most of all, thank you to more than a million households around Australia who have taken a chance on using People Power to tackle their household bills and joined One Big Switch and its sister-platforms over the years.

We don't always get it right, but we do our best and when enough consumers act together, it creates an irrepressible force.

That's why we get up and go to work each day and stories like the ones in this book make it all worthwhile. I hope you make a few of your own and share them with us too.

Go get 'em!